HIGHER *imagination*
A Future for Universities

Ant Bagshaw

Produced for Ant Bagshaw by:

Longueville Media Pty Ltd
PO Box 205 Haberfield NSW 2045
www.longmedia.com.au
info@longmedia.com.au

Copyright © Ant Bagshaw 2023

All rights reserved. Except as permitted under the Copyright Act 1968, (for example, a fair dealing for the purposes of study, research, criticism or review) no part of this book may be reproduced, stored in a retrieval system, or transmitted in any form or by any means without prior written permission from the author. For all enquiries or further information contact: ant@higherimagination.com

While all care has been taken in preparing this book, any errors are the author's own.

ISBN: 978-0-6459557-0-5

Praise for Higher Imagination: A Future for Universities

"In *Higher Imagination: A Future for Universities*, Ant Bagshaw introduces the idea of the joyful university, maintains that universities should enable scope for inefficiency to nurture creativity, and puts forward concrete proposals for how universities can better own the delivery of education as a corporate responsibility. Bagshaw has written a stimulating, provocative and pithy book which combines profound insight with constructive policy proposals. The book deserves to be widely read and closely engaged."

Professor Stuart Corbridge, former Vice-Chancellor and Warden,
Durham University, UK

"An intriguing exploration of the concept of joy to reshape organizational structures and culture. Ant Bagshaw's work is both a valuable and necessary contribution to the public discourse of HE and organisational culture more broadly."

Dr Jennifer Beattie, Head of Government Relations,
Griffith University, Australia

"Ant Bagshaw outlines the need for universities to embrace technology and change, to help shape the way these coming juggernauts will impact HE whilst, at the same time, putting the needs of students and those that serve them at the heart of positive decision-making along with the need for joy in the sector. Ant is someone I always listen to, and this book allows us all to tap into his wealth of knowledge and has some meaningful takeaways which will, I believe, help us in our work serving this amazing, vibrant sector."

Joe Avison, Managing Director Global Relations,
The Chronicle of Higher Education

"A serious and thoughtful book that takes universities and the HE sector as they are, not how we might wish them to be. The reader will immediately grasp why Ant's advice is sought after by university leaders around the world."

Sam Roseveare, Director of Regional and National Policy, University of Warwick, UK

"Ant Bagshaw is a leading practitioner in global HE who, more than most of us, understands the need for the time, space and opportunity to think. He thinks deeply and with novelty, added to wisdom arising from his diverse experience. He uses this combination to exercise his imagination and, in this book, his consideration of issues he presents for others to think about in HE is priceless. Ant strikes a fine balance adding novel and insightful ideas for the future in a way that is reconcilable to the way the sector currently operates and is led. The result is an invaluable and truly imaginative agenda, and manifesto for change, that all HE leaders would be wise to add to their own thinking time and space in working out their own plans for the future. I am sure many will become highly enriched through doing so."

Emeritus Professor Martin Betts, former Deputy Vice-Chancellor Engagement, Griffith University, Australia, and Founder at HEDx

"*Higher Imagination: A Future for Universities* is a brilliant and highly accessible capture of the university public policy environment – highly recommended for beginners and experts alike. Ant's inimitable writing style makes this feel like a conversation with a friend, full of warmth and humour. His approach uses authentic storytelling weaved in alongside clear, perceptive insights. As someone who has worked in the HE policy system in both the UK and Australia, I found this to be a superb and concise capture of all things HE including a thoughtful and stimulating vision for the future. A highly enjoyable read for anyone interested in universities and HE policy."

Libby Hackett, CEO, James Martin Institute for Public Policy and Visiting Fellow in Global Higher Education Policy and Funding, Crawford School of Public Policy, Australian National University

For the Aran Mountains and space to think

About the author

Dr Ant Bagshaw works to improve higher education. He started his career at the National Union of Students, UK, and has been a professional staff member at the University of Kent, London School of Economics, and University College London. He joined the influential commentary site Wonkhe in 2016 and became its first Deputy CEO. From 2018 to 2021 he was a management consultant with Nous Group, first in London and then in the company's Australian headquarters in Melbourne. He gave evidence to the Australian Senate as it considered new HE legislation in 2020.

Along the way, Ant was a reviewer with the UK's Quality Assurance Agency for Higher Education, a trustee of charity Student Hubs, a member of the council at the independent HE provider the Dyson Institute of Engineering and Technology, and sales and marketing lead for Online Education Services' UK operation. He currently lives in Sydney where he is a senior strategy consultant in L.E.K. Consulting's Global Education Practice, leading the firm's work in Australia and Aotearoa / New Zealand. He also works internationally, specialising in HE and providing strategic advice for institutions, governments, and businesses.

Ant was an undergraduate at the University of Cambridge, received a PGCE in post-compulsory education and training at Cardiff University, and in 2021 completed an EdD at the University of Sheffield with a thesis titled *Dialogue and consultation in higher education policymaking: a critical policy analysis of the tertiary funding review in England, 2017–2019*. With Wonkhe's Dr Debbie McVitty, he co-edited *Influencing Higher Education Policy: A Professional Guide to Making an Impact*, published by Routledge in 2020. Ant teaches a course on policy influence in HE as Affiliated Faculty at the University of Pennsylvania on its Master of Science in Education programme in Global Higher Education Management.

You can follow Ant's blog at www.higherimagination.com and connect on LinkedIn: www.linkedin.com/in/antbagshaw/.

Acknowledgements

I set out to write a book on the future of HE in mid 2022, sitting at the dining table of a cottage in Wales' Eryri (Snowdonia) National Park. I finished this book sat at my dining table on Gadigal country in Sydney, in mid 2023, having moved to the other side of the world for a new professional adventure. In that time, I tested the developing ideas with many colleagues and friends and I read more of the HE literature across academic work, think tank reports, journalism, and comment. This book is based on my experience working in, and thinking about, the HE sector in the UK and Australia over 15 years in a variety of roles. I have been immersed in HE, am confident that it creates value for society and for individuals, and I know that there is more to be achieved. It is in the spirit of contributing to the rich and stimulating debates about the future of HE that I offer this manifesto on a future for universities.

I would like to thank colleagues, friends, and collaborators from across the sector, and beyond, who helped me to develop the ideas in this book through conversation and in their considered and generous feedback on the emerging ideas. In particular, I thank Anip Sharma, Derfel Owen, Gaia Fassò, James Green, Jennifer Beattie, Jessica Cecil, Joe Avison, Jonathan Grant, Kent Anderson, Libby Hackett, Lucinda Parr, Martin Betts, Michael Englard, Rose Luckin, Sam Roseveare, Stephen Weller, Stuart Corbridge, Sudeep Laad, and Tom Kennie. Adele Tyson provided useful and generous advice throughout the writing process. I thank my mother for introducing me to Bakhtin, amongst other things. I am grateful to the journalists and editors who give me a platform for exploring topical issues in HE, including Anton Crace at *QS Insights*; John Ross at *Times Higher Education*; Julie Hare at the *Australian Financial Review*; and Tim Dodd at *The Australian*. And I would like to thank David Longfield and the team at Longueville Media for helping to bring this project to fruition.

Contents

Prologue | A manifesto for the future university 1

Introduction 4
Take the opportunities in autonomy 18
Make universities joyful 31
Celebrate some inefficiency 41
Treat education as your product 50
Make your research portfolio deliberate 63
Benefit your communities 71
Conclusion 80

Postscript | The future university needs imagination 90

Prologue | A manifesto for the future university

Universities are indispensable platforms to explore ideas, share knowledge, and contribute to social development. They are the products of their histories, the sum of their many and varied parts, and they make decisions and act as institutions. The technological developments which are shaping, and reshaping, our world pose a challenge of to all organisations. The emergence of ubiquitous generative artificial intelligence (AI) looks poised to overhaul society completely. Universities need not to be undone by these new technologies but to be the place where they are embraced, developed, understood, and challenged. Now is the time for universities to seize this moment of change and use its transformational momentum to advance their education, research, and social impact.

We need more graduates. We need people with high-level technical, analytical, and creative skills. Universities are central to meeting that demand for highly skilled people able to make positive impacts on the world. As automation fundamentally transforms industries and the nature of work, universities have a duty to prepare the next generation – and to retrain people already in the workforce – to thrive amid this turbulence. It is the skills of adaptability and inventive thinking, and the capacity to navigate increasingly complex challenges, which are needed now more than ever. Universities must be the educational institutions which respond to this challenge and unlock ever greater human potential.

The market will not solve for this challenge. In a world of instant gratification, on-demand everything, and where cash is king, universities have an opportunity to do more than simply that which markets dictate. There is room for public-purpose organisations which are unshackled by the need for shareholders to profit, or by the need to demonstrate performance for a quarterly return. Unbound by these constraints, universities can dare to do difficult, complicated, risky, and unprofitable things. Their commitment to the mission of education, research, and social impact is the foundation for expansive and life-changing learning, revolutionary discoveries, innovative solutions to otherwise intractable problems, and positive results for communities, locally and globally. If we are going to address the climate emergency, alleviate poverty, and address inequality, or deliver the best life outcomes for everyone, we need universities. Not alone, not without businesses, governments, and other non-profits, but we need them in the intellectual and practical ecosystem. This is an ideal worth keeping for the greater good: our universities have a proud history on which we should build, not compete out of existence.

Now is a time for change. Public-purpose universities have never been more essential. But they face major challenges, including political pressure, the need to achieve more with less, and an accelerating pace of change. Universities are institutions which have protected themselves by being conservative and slow to change. Rather than dwell in the present, the case for change needs to focus on what will be the achievements of the future. My vision for the future university means that:

- they demonstrate, through their institutional leadership in society, the undeniable benefit that their existence has for each and every person
- they are places of joyful work in which every member of the community is valued, respected, and has the platform to do their best work
- as learning organisations, they use the tools of inquiry and experimentation to become better every day
- in everything they do, particularly education and research, they seek both good absolute outcomes and equitable access to those outcomes for students, staff, and communities
- they are thoughtful in their use of resources to maximise the benefits that can be achieved in delivery of their mission
- they balance effective collaboration and considered challenge to ensure that they work effectively with other alike and different organisations, and that they hold true to their values in the ways that they work

Radical change may be difficult, even scary. It may also be the exciting and vital activity which ensures that the university's mission is not only achieved now but secured for future generations. We have the power to change universities for good. Let's use it.

Introduction

Change from the inside: the case for joyful universities

I first met Dr Jonathan Nicholls when I became one of the student members of the Council at the University of Cambridge when he was at the beginning of his time there as Registrary, an archaic term for the University's chief operating officer. Many of our interactions were fraught. There was constant, albeit fairly low-level, tension between the Students' Union and the administrative centre of Cambridge, the aptly named Old Schools. We were campaigning for progress – at least that which we thought of as progress at the time – in an institution seemingly incapable of change. I remember difficult conversations with Jonathan. But he was a gentleman, always polite and professional, and not one to shy away from challenge when it was often needed.

In his manner, and in his actions, Jonathan taught me a lot about what it was to be the professional in a university's professional services. When we met again a decade or so later, when I was at the media organisation Wonkhe, and he at law firm Shakespeare Martineau, I found Jonathan generous, creative, and full of energy for the betterment of the HE sector. Jonathan died in March 2022. In his memory, his friends and colleagues at the UK's Association of Heads of University Administration created an essay prize in his honour with the prompt:

Higher Education Reimagined: Identify one innovative idea that would transform HE institutions for the better and consider how we make it happen in practice.

I was inspired to write an essay – happily, shortlisted for the prize – which developed an emerging idea of the need for more joy in universities. Joy is a deliberately provocative word, not one usually deployed in a work context. Through this provocation I aimed to prompt reflection on what it means for every individual working in the sector to find – or at least have the conditions or capacity to find – joy in their work. I hope that Jonathan would have appreciated the spirit with which that essay was intended: enabling the best from the professional requires care for the personal.

Creating joy in HE institutions will make the sector a better place. Our marketised HE system has some positive dimensions, not least the success of massification in widening participation beyond a narrow elite.[1] But the system also has many well-documented failings which have eroded positive elements of working in, and for, the sector. Managerialism has been accompanied by a financial focus with too great an emphasis on efficiency of inputs over positive outcomes. There is a need for joy to redress this balance and prioritise humanity in HE. This book supports redressing that balance by offering approaches and solutions which recognise the constraints in which universities operate and prompt humane responses. Creating and leading joyful institutions will not be easy, but the actions taken to get there will be more than worth the effort.

The world is changing, and universities need to change too

In spite of the great success of HE and its core institutions – universities – over many centuries, the sector can be no exception from the need to understand, and respond to, the changing needs in society beyond universities. There are

---

1 The role of the market, or marketisation, in HE is well-explored in the sector's literature, most often with a focus on its negative impacts. The development and implementation of market approaches is bound up with concepts of neoliberalism and new public management. For a pithy summary of the issue, the review of post-18 funding in England (the Augar Review of 2019) says: 'Post-18 education cannot be left entirely to market forces. The idea of a market in tertiary education has been a defining characteristic of English policy since 1998. We believe that competition between providers has an important role to play in creating choice for students but that on its own it cannot deliver a full spectrum of social, economic and cultural benefits. With no steer from government, the outcome is likely to be haphazard.'

some very obvious changes and disruptions affecting HE, not least the recent transformational impact of the COVID pandemic on all elements of personal and professional life. But there are much broader and deeper trends of disruption, in technologies including generative AI, the changing nature of the workplace, or in society, culture, and politics. Without continuous adaptation, universities risk losing their position as the institutions by which society achieves positive outcomes through education and research. Politicians and commentators decry poor value for money in out-of-touch ivory towers captured by the 'workerati'. Academics complain of precarious contracts, excessive workloads, and reducing benefits. Students are frustrated by all too slow action on institutional racism, sexual harassment, and support for mental health. It is too easy to paint a picture of a sector facing crises on many fronts.

There is plenty of material out there which speaks to the crises in universities.[2] It is easy to find in the literature the diagnosis of the problem, and there are thought experiments which offer 'if only the conditions were different' solutions to the ills facing the sector. There is value in these contributions to the discourse about the future of HE, so I aim not to repeat those approaches but to build on them. From my experiences as a student, and from my career working in the sector, I know that universities are enormously valuable. I also know that that is not just a historical position, and they continue to create value for people as individuals, particularly as students, and collectively as a society. I seek universities which are set up to maximise the value they create and the positive impact that they have on the world. I want a thriving sector, and so I offer a proposition for a future university which, using a little imagination, is able to do good within the constraints – and freedoms – of the prevailing regulatory conditions.

Is there really a big problem to solve?

It is lazy just to accept the premise that universities are in a perma-crisis and that we must upend the whole system to achieve different conditions and better results. If we take a longer view, universities are places where many people – particularly academic staff on open-ended contracts and professional staff

---

2 Recent books include *English universities in crisis: Markets without competition* by Frank, Gowar and Naef (Bristol University Press, 2019) and Peter Scott's *Retreat or resolution? Tackling the crisis of mass higher education* (Policy Press, 2021). Paul Ashwin's *Transforming university education: A manifesto* (Bloomsbury Academic, 2020) provides a useful summary of the many and various crises which have been observed in HE, and he fittingly calls his introductory chapter 'Not another book about the higher education crisis!'.

– find both meaningful employment and good pay and conditions. The focus on community engagement, innovation and knowledge exchange has made universities more impactful. Similarly, students have access to healthcare services, careers advice, accommodation and other student support mechanisms which were not available to previous generations. We should celebrate that which is good now, and note that universities have been good at adapting slowly to the changing external conditions. The HE sector can muddle along, shaped incrementally by innovation and market pressure. But this approach is not sufficient for realising the full potential of HE. We need a new vision for universities.

***

In late 2022, the Australian Government announced a review process called the Universities Accord.[3] Since then, naturally, the HE sector in Australia has been consumed by debate about the options for the future of the sector and what should change for the better – for their preferred definition of better, of course. But at the heart of the challenge for the Accord process is an absence of a stated set of problems that reform could solve, or perhaps an unwillingness to name the problems out loud. In response to a frustration about the absence of the problem definition, I offer my own diagnosis, which applies not just to Australia but to the UK's universities too, as they operate in sufficiently similar conditions and have shared histories.

1. **Universities expect too much from governments**
   Brought out starkly in the debate on the Universities Accord, the 'answer' for the sector too often lies in 'If only we had more money, we would be better'. It is entirely possible that greater resources would make for a better HE sector, but focussing on this ask of government misses the practical and political realities that there is no more money for universities. As the need for higher-level skills increases, so governments are keen to ensure participation in HE. But they are not keen on a greater share of the national budget going to universities, not least because there isn't enough voter interest in it. In general, what happens in, or for, universities is not salient in the political debate in the way that policy issues elsewhere in education can be, particularly schools. In response, universities need to make the most of the opportunities

---

3 For a primer on the Universities Accord, see 'Don't Look Back at Augar: The purpose of policy reviews in higher education', which I wrote for *QS Insights* 01, https://magazine.qs.com/qs-insights-magazine-01/headlines-policy-reviews.

which their quasi-autonomy allows to shape their own destinies.[4] This is the central premise of the book: one of the distinctively exciting things about universities is their capacity to build their own destinies within the broad frameworks which governments provide. They can, and must, do their best to help shape those parameters, but, fundamentally, they need to work within the parameters which they are given.

2. **Working conditions in HE aren't good enough**
Complaints from staff that the universities are places of precarious work, that demands are ever increasing, and that poor behaviours are left unaddressed are often justified. These features of working life in the contemporary university are, in part, a consequence of too great a focus on narrow performance measures and too little on the human side of what makes universities special. The focus on short-term outcomes for students, and through pressure to produce ever-more research, has come at too great a cost. There is insufficient emphasis on the longer-term benefits which could come from happier and healthier workplaces. This gap needs to be addressed through a focus on joyful workplaces that promote positive experiences and outcomes for everyone.

3. **There is too much inefficiency in the wrong places**
While many universities have pursued greater efficiency in their operations, too few have sought really to optimise what they do. They are required to respond to the increasing pressure of massified HE – we need more graduates – coupled with limited desire for further investment from taxpayer funds and limits on what can, or should, be contributed by each student. To meet this demand, they need to get better at delivering education. New technologies offer new and exciting potential for greater efficiency, facilitating education and student support. Universities also need to consider the ways in which their mission can be best achieved through different structures to seek to be the size and shape which use limited resources well. But the bind is that universities need, simultaneously, to pursue efficient operations whilst enabling the inefficiency of research in which new ideas can flourish.

---

4 I've used the term 'quasi-autonomy' because I don't see that universities could ever be considered truly autonomous institutions. They are established by governments, highly regulated (which is unlikely to change radically), and with funding for education and research mostly driven by governments one way or another. As such, while they have the capacity to make many independent decisions, there are major limits on what's possible.

4. **Universities are too keen to over-service students**
   Institutional incentives are to recruit as many students as possible, keep them studying for as long as possible, and charge them the maximum they can bear. This core incentive pushes universities to build products around what serves the institution, and not what serves the student. While this approach means responding to the short-term imperatives of the market conditions, there is enormous risk that this undermines universities in the longer term, and makes it harder to deliver on the true mission of education. Universities should take more sophisticated approaches to how they think about their portfolios of education products to ensure that they meet students' needs and are efficiently delivered.

5. **Research is funded too haphazardly**
   Freedom of academic inquiry is vitally important and a feature of universities' success, and essential to the contributions they make to society. But the way universities invest in research – largely through time allocations – is not structured to derive good outcomes. This may not have been a material problem in the past, but it is increasingly a challenge where the economics of universities means that teaching activity and research investment are less and less aligned in the same organisational units. There should, therefore, be a more effective redistributive mechanism, and one which supports a balanced portfolio of research activities. A structured investment approach is needed to enable proportionate investment across disciplines and projects.

6. **Social impact is an afterthought**
   Sometimes described as 'third leg' or 'third stream' activities, social impact is too often an afterthought in universities, not a core part of the mission. This is central to the social contract: institutions are platforms in which education and research take place, and in return for the autonomy with which they can shape those activities, they need to invest directly in benefitting communities through deliberate action, not spill-overs. It is also where the demonstration that universities are more than the sum of their parts comes from; as preservers of knowledge for public good, this area also includes supporting public access to knowledge, artefacts, and resources. A greater focus on the interconnection of social impact with education and research will enable the full realisation of the potential of the future university.

These six problems, each of which is addressed in this book, are underpinned by the need for university leaders – individually and collectively – to seek better outcomes for institutions and the sector as a whole. In many debates, particularly with policymakers and sector commentators, there is lament for the quality of leadership in universities. Inevitably, with a large and diverse sector, this criticism has a mix of truth and unfairness. At the heart of the complaint is that universities have a complex relationship with leadership, with both rewards for leaders – in status and remuneration – and too often disdain for those who seek and take on leadership roles. With insufficient attention to, and investment in, leadership throughout universities, perhaps we get the leaders we deserve. Addressing the problems outlined here offers opportunities to demonstrate the leadership required for the future of universities.

Who is this book for?

It may already be apparent that this book is, selfishly, for me. My experience working in HE, and reading about the sector, is that the literature leaves me wanting more. I may not be the only one frustrated by the literature which espouses a return to some 'good old days' where academics were untroubled by the administration of universities and could go about the high-minded pursuit of research (and teaching if absolutely necessary) untrammelled by any need to pay bills. These golden age elegies fail to reconcile the realities of the situation in which we find ourselves; they seek all the benefits of a luxuriously small sector without asking the question of how this can be afforded alongside mass participation. And perhaps that is the point: their authors, mostly implicitly, but some explicitly, reject the premise that massification is good for the individual and for society. Ultimately, these works fail to provide practical solutions which a contemporary reader working within the present system of HE could act upon.

On the other hand, there are works which present a need for universities to follow the adaptations seen in large businesses, particularly large technology companies. These, too, can be impractical, with too strong a focus on the market dynamics in HE which are only partially in effect. There are strong cultural, economic, and political forces – reinforced by path dependencies – which place universities within the social fabric. These forces will not likely be undone, in the short term at least, by the Netflix-isation of unbundled content or the

Uber-isation of gig economy labour.[5] I am not trying to be a Luddite; there is a lot which universities can learn from other industries, from other countries' systems, and from the broad forces of technological and social disruption. But the task for the leader of a university is to work with the conditions which they have – the opportunities and challenges – to take pragmatic steps for the future of the institution.

Aside from a dissatisfaction with sector commentary, I wanted to write this book out of my own frustration with the missed opportunities that I see in HE. I have worked in and around universities in the UK and Australia, with some brief forays into other countries along the way. I've been a professional staff member in universities, sector commentator, student activist, management consultant, doctoral researcher, governing body member, quality reviewer, and advisor to vice-chancellors. The HE sector has room for debate from many sides, and this book should push the boundaries of thinking about its future.

***

I have framed my argument as a future, not the future, to recognise that it represents a provocation based on a model, rather than a prediction or prescription. I would like it to be read by colleagues across the sector, whether working as leaders of institutions, policymakers, professional staff, or academics, and for it to provide stimulus for their thinking on what makes a successful university. I see an absence of solution-focussed approaches to HE commentary, and I would like to change that. If I set myself a test for this book, it is whether you find in it some ideas which you can imagine might actually be enacted within your professional lifetime, and not in some far-off abstract future. But I am not presenting a guide for how to manage the minutiae of institutional life; I aim to find a connection between the purposes and missions of HE and the practice of leading institutions, something which the management literature may miss.

While I have presented a large potential audience for this book, I also want to make clear that its arguments apply in those contexts that I know best, specifically those systems of HE which have adopted quasi-market approaches with high levels of regulatory control. The UK's four systems have variants on this model, with England the most extreme in its level of contribution from the student. There

---

5 For a contemporary provocation about the potential of technological disruption in HE, see *The New Learning Economy: Thriving beyond higher education* by Martin Betts and Michael Roseman (Routledge, 2023). Exploring how others' innovations and disruptions have been transformational across industries is a vital part of determining what should, and shouldn't, be the way forward in HE.

are many lessons for Australia too. The core principle, which will resonate with colleagues in other systems, like those in Éire / Republic of Ireland, Aotearoa / New Zealand, and Canada, is that the existing level of institutional autonomy provides space for meaningful decisions about purpose and direction but is bounded by a need to deliver a broad public good. This is not to make the case for relative merits of the quasi-market against a more free-market model or state-controlled approach, but to start with the realities of the model as it stands.

The book is about the non-profit HE providers, often described in common parlance as 'public' but sitting at arm's length from the true public sector. I have used these universities as the framing for the book, not to exclude the value that other providers of HE offer but to focus the effort on the future for those many institutions which have a problem to solve. Rather than focus on a subset of those public universities, I have adopted an inclusive approach which assumes that all do add value, and all can do better. Universities, be they ancient or brand new, large or small, face a fundamental problem of relevance to society. They have been found wanting by staff, by students, and by politicians and policymakers. Institutional leaders might reasonably say that the so-called problem of expensive education, worsening pay and conditions, and/or limited positive impact on students' life outcomes may be the direct result of policy measures, or other exogenous factors outside the control of providers. But those arguments are irrelevant. Many others have called this situation a crisis; my interpretation is that this is not a crisis as in an emergency or a short-term problem, but is a chronic long-term set of connected issues about how universities can find, and deliver upon, their purpose.

Where does imagination come into it?

Imagination is both a practical tool and an indulgent one. If there is a chronic problem to solve – the connection of purpose to action in mass HE systems – then stepping back to ask what might be better requires an exercise in imaginative thinking. In the most basic sense, the idea is that we should all be willing and able to imagine possible futures with some features the same, and some different, from our current condition. The title is also a nod to Mikhail Bakhtin's *The Dialogic Imagination*. I am taken by the principle of dialogic engagement and meaning-making through the intersection of words (Bakhtin's interanimation), and with the aspiration for continued making and re-making of meaning:

> *There is neither a first nor a last word and there are no limits to the dialogic context (it extends into the boundless past and the boundless future). Even past meanings, that is, those born in the dialogue of the past centuries, can never be stable (finalized, ended once and for all) – they will always change (be renewed) in the process of subsequent, future development in the dialogue. At any moment in the development of the dialogue there are immense, boundless masses of forgotten contextual meanings, but at certain moments of the dialogue's subsequent development along the way they are recalled and invigorated in renewed form (in a new context). Nothing is absolutely dead: every meaning will have its homecoming festival.*[6]

There is an interpretation of imagination which implies a fanciful exploration of futures for the sector. I propose imagination in moderation: I seek new and positive futures for universities which build upon their histories, cultures, and values. But I also want to offer challenge by considering how strong incentives can push colleagues to the breaking point, and which do not always serve the needs of students or other stakeholders. This is imagination for exploration with realism for the connection of those indulgent possibilities to practical realities. In taking this approach, I hope that others' imaginations may be sparked to consider alternative positive futures for the sector. It is, therefore, in the spirit of dialogue that this book is presented to the reader. In making this written contribution to the HE debate, itself informed by the literature, I make an offering to the discourse. And, with it, invite others to imagine, and to engage, comment, and critique. When read and interpreted in the reader's own context, the book may have meaning.

Imagination as a tool for exploring ideas should, I hope, also serve the reader who is already a leader in the university to put aside some assumptions. The demands of university leadership often focus on the time in office, on what can be achieved in a five- or seven-year term. I invite the imagination which looks ahead to what the successful institution will be in a century's time. How can all of the university's assets – intellectual, physical, financial, reputational – be protected and enhanced over the long term by decisions made today? While the external conditions of a century ahead will be very different, it is reasonable to assume that education and research remain core. And if they are not, we may either be the poorer as a society for their absence, or much the richer from their replacement

---

6 M M Bakhtin, *Speech genres and other late essays* (eds. C Emerson and M Holquist; trans. V W McGee), University of Texas Press Slavic series, Vol. 8, Austin: University of Texas Press, p. 170, 1986.

by something better. But I will leave these to science fiction and work on the premise that the core purpose of the university remains valuable. This book is set squarely on using imagination to understand better how the core mission of the university can be strengthened, and not just through initiatives but through the structures, policy settings, and incentives which might provide the resilience for even greater long-term success. And, as with all imaginative exercises, the answer may not be the right one, but it could spark other ideas.

What is this book not about?

My future for universities is deliberately constrained to describing core principles for HE and making proposals for how they can better be delivered. But there are inevitably many constraints on what it is possible to explore in this subset of the HE discourse. First, this book isn't going to cover the histories of the sector which are well covered elsewhere[7]: the histories are vitally important for understanding where we are now, how we got here, and where HE has been valuable in the past. These histories also reveal the origins of the path dependencies which may constrain future action. In choosing not to retell the history, I am leaving this task to others who have already told the stories better than I will, and I am also suggesting that too great a focus on the past might limit our imaginative capacity for the future. My attention is on making the best of the situation we have now with a view to setting out positive near-term futures which provide the conditions for long-term success.

There is an obverse to the omission of the history section, which is too great a focus on abstract futures. There are many accounts of the future which make the case that others from outside, particularly large technology companies, will come for that which is good about the sector and leave universities as shrivelled husks of their former glory.[8] I am not going to present that assessment of the challenge

....

7 The Australian HE sector is well covered by Glyn Davis in *The Australian idea of a university* (Melbourne University Press, 2017) and Hannah Forsyth in *A history of the modern Australian university* (NewSouth, 2014). For the UK, Peter Scott's *Retreat or resolution?* (Policy Press, 2021) provides a good explanation of how we got to the system we have and could be read alongside Michael Shattock's *Making policy in British higher education 1945–2011* (Open University Press/McGraw Hill, 2012) and David Willetts' *A university education* (Oxford University Press, 2017). Miguel Urquiola in *Markets, minds and money: Why America leads the world in university research* (Harvard University Press, 2021) provides an interesting assessment of the US's development contrasted with European models. Readers looking to delve further will find in these works the references to the 'origin story' texts for the sector, which explore more foundational questions.

8 Famously in the UK, the 2013 report from the Institute of Public Policy Research *An avalanche is coming: Higher education and the revolution ahead* predicted that major disruption would come from Massive Open Online Courses (MOOCs). While these courses grew in the decade which

for the sector because I believe that there remains a need for the universities which we have to find renewed purpose to serve the future of HE. Universities are there to serve greater needs than those which the market will fund. There is a point to having universities, to establishing them and supporting them through direct and indirect public funds, and that is to create benefit with that investment. And it is reasonable to do that in a not-for-profit setting where the mission of the institution is to do as much good as possible for as many people as possible within whatever limited resources it has. In that, and in the dedication of those who serve the mission of universities, there is a lot for all of us to be proud.

I'm going to avoid, where possible, speaking to the differentiation of the sector by rankings or other notions of prestige. As others have written, there are many issues with ranking systems, from the profit-seeking motives of those who compile them to the quality of data used to engineer them, and to the problem of their zero-sum nature, which means there will always be many more losers than winners.[9] My starting point is that all universities have value, and all can deliver greater positive impact, whatever their starting base of financial resources, intellectual capital, or reputation may be. This approach also follows from exploring a future of HE within highly regulated systems which have high expectations for all universities, not just focussing on a rarefied elite.

While I share some anecdotes about individual universities, I have chosen not to prioritise examples of practices or institutions to illustrate my points. There is always a risk in highlighting good practices that one does not know the whole story. Whether we are within or outside an institution, our assessment of the merits and failings of an approach or initiative is limited. There is also risk in focussing too much on practice today which distracts from potential futures. The omission of detailed examples is therefore deliberate. But I recognise that there are many examples of interesting and creative practice upon which I could draw to make my points from the systems that I know best and from other places around the world. Our universities are innovative and adaptive places. They are good at learning from each other, benchmarking performance, and sharing their successes. For my imagined future, I take this rich collage of the universities we have now to inform my view but I seek not to be anchored to any practice or institution.

---

followed the report, MOOCs did not herald the complete unbundling of the university education. While much derided for that point, its essential message of the need for change in universities will resonate with a contemporary reader.

9 See, for example, former vice-chancellor Chris Brink's *The Soul of a University: Why excellence is not enough* (Bristol University Press, 2021).

HE is not the be-all-and-end-all of education, not even of education at the levels universities traditionally teach. For many, the education which they receive in the vocational sector will be superior to universities for its professional relevance and quality of teaching. Equally, apprenticeships, which in England have seen significant recent growth in the degree-level segment, provide educational and professional opportunities which have positive transformational effects on learners' lives. It is possible, and vitally important, to celebrate that which is positive about HE while recognising the value that other sectors provide. There are also opportunities in more connected tertiary systems, in new ways of accessing HE which have strong industry engagement, and in developing non-HE institutions. But the recognition of the value elsewhere does not solve the problems that face our public-purpose universities, which this book aims to tackle.

***

I will speak to students as consumers of education. This does not have to be a disempowering conception of their role: it can be entirely consistent with a partnership approach. While students and alumni exist as a strong component within the exploration of futures, my approach is to question, from the institutional side, what structures and incentives are most likely to generate the greatest benefit. I will not explore the experiences of any particular group; I think that it is incumbent on institutions to work within the constraints provided to them by the regulated quasi-market system to serve everyone, and with a view to pursuit of the greatest equity in activity and outcomes.

I'm also going to avoid a discussion on the funding of HE. Funding HE is a hot topic of debate, but one which is largely a distraction from the core task that I am presenting: the need to work within the constraints provided. There are clearly material issues in the ways students access loans to fund their study, issues for the taxpayer and issues for the individual.[10] The debate around the Job Ready Graduates package of measures in Australia shows that it is hard to find a 'right' or 'fair' answer in a system which aims to grow student numbers in the same resource envelope, and to incentivise different behaviours for students and institutions. On the research and capital side, it is also tricky to find the balance between block grants and competitive schemes. While these are all important

---

10   While now a bit dated, there is a lot to be learned about university funding from Andrew McGettigan in *The great university gamble: Money, markets and the future of higher education* (Pluto Press, 2013), in Roger Brown and Helen Carasso's *Everything for sale? The marketisation of UK higher education* (Routledge 2013), and in David Willetts' *Issues and ideas on higher education: Who benefits? Who pays?* (King's College London, 2015).

and valuable debates, the primary task for leaders and governors of universities is to see what they can do with the models as presented to them, how to optimise within the given conditions.

I believe that universities should influence that system for the better, but the pragmatism in this book comes from an acceptance of the broad terms of the conditions presented to the sector and the need to work within those for the greatest possible positive outcomes. Just as this book isn't going to offer policymakers a shopping list of policy recommendations, it is not a how-to guide for leadership and management of universities. It should inform leaders, as it informs policymakers, but the reader will find more broad principles than detailed activities.

How is the book structured?

This is a two-part book. In the first part, I take broad principles by which future universities should be run. These follow the first three problems outlined above in the role of autonomy, promoting joy, and operating with a balance of efficiency and inefficiency. I make the case that for the future university to work – to achieve its mission – it needs to embrace these underlying principles.

The following three chapters tackle the core missions of the university: first, education; then, research; and, finally, social impact. I argue that education needs to be highly productised to reach the levels of efficiency and quality of delivery required by students. This approach is also necessary if universities are going to compete successfully with alternative models of education or skills development, and to deliver surpluses for reinvestment. In the chapter on research, I advance the case that research needs to be supported to succeed through a risk-weighted investment model which provides the space and time to deliver high-quality outputs. And I explore how social impact can be core business, not an afterthought.

Each chapter aims to offer a clear proposition for an element of the future of the university. While they could be taken in isolation – and, typically, I expect universities would pick and choose elements for their strategies – my goal is to present a set of ideas which, taken together, present connected and coherent conditions for a successful future university. I offer these ideas as a prompt for further dialogic engagement about the future of HE.

Take the opportunities in autonomy

Universities are amazing, complex, networked organisations. If we are to have imaginative responses to shape the future of HE, we need first to explore the purposes of the university and the environment in which they currently operate. Universities aim to provide high quality education and research while doing good in the world, making a greater contribution through institutional existence than simply the sum of their many activities. The marketised systems of HE currently create clear, if too blunt and sometimes unhelpful, incentives for institutional behaviour. The task of institutional leaders and their strategies is to recognise the power of these incentives and to find ways to shape them, using the gifts of autonomy and the distinctive capabilities of the university, to achieve the mission of HE.

Universities exist to do good for individuals and for society

Universities play a unique and multifaceted role in society, with the potential to be catalysts for social mobility, cultural advancement, and economic prosperity. For those who work in the sector, the core appeal of the university often lies in the intangible mix of intellectual freedom and societal contribution that universities offer. Universities are spaces for rigorous enquiry, for the joy of discovering and imparting knowledge, and the satisfaction of shaping the thinkers and doers of the next generation. But all this needs to be paid for.

In the operation of the university, there is a delicate balance between purpose and financial sustainability: universities need both the freedom to pursue their unique purpose and the financial means to make these ambitions a reality. This is not just about keeping the lights on; it's about fostering an environment that allows for the exploration of ideas, the creation of conditions for intellectual and creative joy, and the ability to impact lives positively. It's about maintaining the vitality that fuels the people whose vocation is to work in HE.

The benefits of HE are both large and well distributed across both public and private spheres. On an individual level, students benefit from the skills, knowledge, and credentials that a university education provides, enhancing their career prospects and personal development. For society, the benefits are equally profound: research drives innovation and informs policy, graduates contribute to the workforce and the economy, and the cultural and community engagement of universities enriches society. Moreover, these institutions also serve as a nexus for cross-cultural exchange, a place to explore and challenge ideas, and to foster civic responsibility.

Creating an HE system which serves, in perpetuity, the diverse needs of taxpayers, staff, and students may seem like an insurmountable task. Is it asking too much to pursue all of these goals at once? The key to success lies in recognising and respecting the differentiated purposes of universities so that the system works in aggregate. Not all universities need to, or should, have the same targets or strategy. Embracing the diversity of these institutions and their respective roles within the wider ecosystem of HE is vital. Such a system requires thoughtful policy guidance, an appreciation of institutional diversity, and strategic investment.

The unrestricted open market is insufficiently good at fulfilling the rich diversity of purposes which universities are expected to deliver, and in all the places that they need to exist. We need universities if we are going to tackle the scourges of society, including the climate crisis, inequality, and health emergencies. Of course, private enterprise, dedicated research organisations, and government agencies are also needed. Where universities fit in is in providing platform capabilities which are not present in those other organisations. It is the multi-faceted and multi-connected ways of working in universities, using the triple helix of education, research, and social impact, which makes their contribution distinctly and positively different to those of the other organisations.

In essence, universities represent a microcosm of society's hopes and dreams, serving as a bridge between knowledge and its practical application. Their mission is to facilitate the betterment of individuals and societies, and, in doing so, they continually strive to balance the joy of intellectual pursuit with the pragmatic necessity of financial sustainability. By recognising the unique role each institution plays in this endeavour, we can envisage an HE sector which brings enduring value for everyone.

In defence of the irrational

I am regularly presented with arguments which say that the university as we know it is not long for this world. Universities are too ossified, too unwilling to face the realities of the contemporary economy, or so the argument goes. The product is bad – too expensive, not relevant enough – so of course it will be competed out of existence. Sometimes these arguments are associated with the idea that all learning can be atomised into micro-credentials which any student can access anywhere in the world at any time.

This argument was crystallised for me by a colleague convinced that the poor quality of education in a large and prominent institution at which his partner was studying would inevitably mean that it would be disrupted out of existence. How can the system survive if the quality is so low? But the reality is that these arguments – grounded in a rational economic model and relying on treating a university education just like any other service – fail to account for the deeply irrational dimensions of the role of universities. To continue to advocate for the existence of universities, we should recognise that these irrational dimensions exist, and that we may need to challenge them.

- **High-prestige professions hire graduates.** Almost every politician, judge, banker, journalist, captain of industry, and so on, studied in at least one university. While there are people who make it into highly paid and prominent positions without degrees, they are the exception, rather than the norm. Attending university will continue to be perceived as a primary route to status and success.
- **University brands matter.** There is enormous intangible value in association with a university. Just as luxury goods have value beyond the materials used to make them, or original artworks have more value than facsimiles, we are all complicit in ascribing prestige to universities. The pomp, traditions, buildings, and imagery all add to this affinity. And it's not just one's own university which is important: we value universities in general, because tarnishing one would undermine the implicit value in our association to another institution.

- **It's hard to substitute once you've started.** Students are incentivised to forgive the issues within their universities, such as poor-quality learning and teaching, because they've made their choice and cannot, in most practical senses, change their mind. Even with the prospects of credit transfer between institutions, there is a sunk cost in having started at one institution and then needing to start afresh elsewhere. Unless a course is wholly online, moving one's physical location is also a barrier to changing institutions. The inclination is to make it work, in spite of any negative reality.
- **University remains a rite of passage**. Not all education is done for the purely instrumental reason of gaining credentials. Attending a university remains an attractive experience for many, a chance to explore ideas, meet people, be challenged, and benefit from facilities and networks. With longer working lives ahead, attending university as a full-time post-school experience makes even more sense. A period of intensive study is also a time of 'learning to learn', which enables graduates to take advantage of lifelong learning opportunities.

These points shouldn't imply that every experience should be a full-time residential mode for school-leavers. The affiliation factors exist for every student, and universities need to be places where mature learners find supportive environments which fit around the other features of their lives. The essence is that, holistically, rather than for any individual experience, the position of universities is entrenched in social norms and expectations.

The irrational value in universities illuminates the disconnect between the idea of the educational experience as the primary transaction with the university and the reality that there is much more about going to, or studying in, university. It is these intangibles which are so important to the persistence and longevity of institutions. This position for our contemporary university experience also introduces risk: if we think that students will continue to come in spite of poor quality, we fail to fulfil our mission. If universities focus on branding over substance, they miss the point of being institutions of public purpose. The task is to acknowledge that these intangible benefits of association exist, that there is a value in universities beyond the transaction of education delivery. We cannot become lazy or negligent, relying on past glories to sustain the position of the future university.

Incentive structures limit the good achieved by the system

If universities are so wonderful, and they create benefits for graduates and society, and we are all complicit in turning a blind eye to any issues, what's the problem? The reality is that while HE genuinely does provide these benefits, it is creaking at the seams. There is a need to deliver more – more graduates, more research, more social impact – with limited resources. The current incentives are misaligned for the delivery of consistently good outcomes. The basic economics of universities in the current system is to maximise the recruitment, retention, and fee levels of students and use any and all surplus to pay for research. At the macro level, across the whole sector, this broadly appears to be working. But when we look at the experiences of students and staff, it is clear that the system does not work for everyone. We can hold these two contradictory concepts at the same time: we're hitting the targets but missing the point. Let's have a system which works for all the beneficiaries, and does so both individually and in aggregate.

At the heart of the problem is a fundamental misalignment of the activities and target benefits. On the one hand, education is weighted to the benefit to the individual. They receive their education as an individual experience – with others, yes, but it is a personal journey of learning and development. The certificate has the student's name on it, and they can take their credential wherever they go. There is also the transaction: the student has paid, not only through a financial mechanism but also through the allocation of their time to studying, time which is limited and could have been spent elsewhere. In contrast, the benefits of research are social. For the researcher, while their name will also be on the output of research and they will therefore gain personal portability of the esteem associated with a publication, the point of research is to contribute to something greater. That may be the field or discipline, it may be in public policy, or through applied innovation. The point is that the idea will have a life beyond the researcher, whereas the student's education exists only with them and what they do with it.

We therefore have a problem of competing incentives. How do these manifest?

- **Attracting students is more important than almost anything else.** Universities' first priority is to recruit students; then, their effort is to retain them. Once in, there are practical and emotional barriers to leaving. There is almost zero incentive to ensure either that those students have a positive experience while studying or they achieve positive post-graduation outcomes. Efforts have been made to redress this balance through surveys like Quality Indicators for Learning and Teaching (QILT) in Australia or the

National Student Survey (NSS) in the UK, which then inform students about the educational experience. The development of the Teaching Excellence and Student Outcomes Framework (TEF) in England was a laudable attempt to try to get institutions to focus on their education, but its poor use of data sources, overly simplistic outcome statements, and biases in favour of traditional university hierarchies shows how difficult it is to crack this nut.

- **The emphasis on research diverts from effort on teaching and learning.** The experience for many students – particularly those studying at the highest-prestige, research-intensive universities – is often poor. There is often demonstrably little interest in students' educational experience because staff have such strong incentives, in the form of personal prestige, progression, and promotion, to put discretionary effort into research. And there is good logic to this: for students, the value of their credential is, in large part, a function of the prestige of the institution which is driven by research as reflected in rankings and prizes. Every marginal bit of effort the university puts into research may be at the expense of a student's education but ultimately benefits them in the long run.
- **There are no prizes for community engagement.** The economics of universities are built around education and research, leaving little, if any, incentives to seek greater social impact. There have been efforts through research evaluation mechanisms – Engagement and Impact in Australia's Excellence in Research for Australia (ERA) exercise, and Impact in the UK's Research Excellence Framework (REF) – to place greater emphasis on the applications of research, but these do not address the broader question of the positive impact which the institution can have on its communities. The absence of incentives here means that universities fail to live up to their full potential, with social impact a lesser priority.

The task for leaders in HE is to recognise that these core incentives exist, and that they also create barriers to the full realisation of the benefits which institutions can achieve.

There are no 'good old days' to which we can return

Mass HE is a joy to behold. Among the wealthy OECD countries, the UK ranks eighth, with 57.7% of 25–34-year-olds having experienced tertiary education, and Australia is only three places behind, at 55.9%. At the top of the table is

South Korea, at 69.6%.[11] With students participating in HE in such large volumes, the systems consequentially place large calls on national budgets. Where commentators argue for bygone eras of HE with generously funded institutional allocating grants, rather than following the incentives of the marketised system, they make the case either for HE to take a disproportionately large share of the national budget or for a much smaller system using the same resource more concentrated. In the peculiarly English discourse on HE, this generally boils down to a sense that the universities of Cambridge and Oxford are the only 'proper' universities and that the expansion of the system from the 1830s onwards has been a disaster.[12]

The commentary on what makes a 'good' university betrays the ignorance that there is value to be found across the whole spectrum of contemporary universities. After I first graduated from the hyper-luxury privileged end of the HE system, the University of Cambridge, my eyes were opened by two formative experiences. The first was working at the UK's National Union of Students, and the second was becoming a student reviewer with the UK's Quality Assurance Agency for Higher Education. Both experiences meant that I travelled to, spent time learning about, and immersed myself in the full richness of HE. I saw students having difficult and unpleasant experiences at research-intensive universities which are members of the Russell Group,[13] and similarly bad experiences in under-funded colleges of further education (FE). But I also saw exceptional quality at other FE colleges, some of the best I've ever encountered, and brilliant experiences at teaching-focussed universities and in pockets at other research-intensives. We are not going to fund every institution to the level of resource achieved by the

....

11   2022 data from *Education at a Glance*, Organisation for Economic Cooperation and Development.

12   The 600-year head start offered to these two universities gives them some major compounding advantages: while being comparatively small in student numbers, they regularly receive around half of the sector's annual philanthropic income. Oxford University Press and Cambridge University Press and Assessment are major financial contributors to the universities too, providing them with significant flexibility for how they invest in attracting researcher talent and providing exceptional facilities. While I am very fond of both institutions, it is essential to recognise that their unusual position means that constant comparisons to their position are largely unhelpful for the creative debate on the future for universities.

13   For my views on the Russell Group, see Wikipedia: 'Ant Bagshaw from the Wonkhe think-tank has criticised the use of Russell Group membership as a proxy for selectivity in official Department for Education reports and statistics, as better measures of selectivity are available from UCAS data. He states that the idea that "Russell Group membership is synonymous with 'best'" is "persistent, but unverified". He also notes that this may lead to less scrutiny of the performance of non-Russell Group selective universities with respect to widening participation and improving access.'

medieval universities, but we do the sector no favours with lazy assumptions of what constitutes 'good' or 'bad'.

The task as I see it is to acknowledge the histories of our universities, including the bits we are less proud of, as one source of inspiration for how those institutions should operate in the future. But we also accept that mass HE is here to stay, and is vital for our present and future economies and societies.

Universities need free cash to re-invest for good

I was once told by a seasoned deputy vice-chancellor that it was much easier to manage a university that was growing than one that was contracting. The resource allocation process within the university is always more straightforward when there is a large surplus to distribute, particularly in times when you might end up with an unseemly large amount left over at the end of the year. Universities have been good at conserving their resources, and at managing their assets with a long-term view, enabling the investment in capital, particularly large estates projects. Where they have been less successful, in the main, is in knowing exactly which parts of the institution deliver the surplus and making deliberate and planned choices about when and how to re-invest that bounty into the mission of the university. It is that allocation of the resource which is how universities do good – how they fulfil their broad charitable missions – and therefore why it is so important, first, to maximise the amount for reinvestment and, second, to make informed and purposeful choices about where and how to spend the money.

Much of what universities do in the marketised systems is tightly controlled: they provide a public service under reasonably strict conditions around the prices which can be charged and the service levels which should be achieved, and the broad quality and standards of the academic awards they deliver. The reality, though, is that these conditions are not a full prescription of how education should be offered or research organised, but broad enough to provide freedoms for the university to pursue its own distinctive path. And when it comes to surplus generation, universities are also able – and encouraged – to generate revenue for reinvestment in their missions. The primary sources of 'high margin' return on tuition for universities comes from international student fees, and then the return from premium fees at the postgraduate level, with further flexibility coming from undergraduate programmes which are efficient to deliver.

It is often argued that the cost of tuition to students should be broadly based on the cost of delivery of that education. This is a reasonable proposition, not least one which would avoid the charge of profiteering on the delivery of public services. However, this cost-plus pricing model is inconsistent with the marketised regulatory system. In these systems, it is important for universities to pursue value-based pricing strategies which focus on pricing in relation to the value delivered to the consumer, the student who benefits from the education.

One point of having universities at all is for the mechanism to invest in those activities, particularly research and social impact, in which the private sector would not invest. It is the bounty of the marketised education system to be able to generate cash for thoughtful and deliberate reinvestment, rather than simply wait for a taxpayer handout. It is this free cash which makes universities not just service delivery organisations under contract to government but flexible and creative places able to assert their own missions, choosing where and how to emphasise the parts that they need at any given time. It means that they can do inefficient or unpopular things and take greater risks.

Institutions should shape the sector for the better

The market system and its quasi-autonomy for institutions also enables them to take positions on how the sector should or could be better. That does not mean rejecting wholesale the conditions which are provided, but shaping and reshaping the system to be better. In these marketised systems, there are regular opportunities to contribute to the debates about how the system should be structured. In Australia, the Universities Accord review process provides a great example of how universities should engage with policy development, balancing their ambitions for change with the practical realities of what's possible.

> **Where's the value in the Accord?**[14]
>
> If we temper our ambitions for the review process, leading to major change in the sector, is there still value in the process? I think that it's an essential task to engage and to maintain the optimism that there might be change if also being realistic that it's not guaranteed. Here's my advice for making the most of this year of the Accord:

---

14   This is an excerpt from an essay I wrote for *QS Insights* 01 entitled 'Don't Look Back at Augar'. For a more in-depth exploration of universities' opportunities for influence, see *Influencing Higher Education Policy: A professional guide for making an impact*, edited by Ant Bagshaw and Debbie McVitty (Routledge, 2020).

Assume that there's no extra money. It's tempting to look at a review process and imagine what could change for the HE sector from additional investment. There isn't going to be any more money for the sector. This isn't because the sector isn't valuable or important, or even that there isn't a good case for investment. There won't be extra money because of the macro conditions, because of paying off the borrowing in the pandemic years and focussing extra dollars on sectors which need the money more urgently. In this context, ideas for the Accord need to offer savings, be cost neutral, or very cheap. Ideas for reforming or reorganising the sector to be more efficient are likely to be welcomed by policymakers.

Share your proposals publicly. Teams in universities and other organisations have been working on their documentation for the Accord, and many have shared their responses. But there is more that can be done to communicate about the themes and issues raised and actively debated with stakeholders, and not just published on websites. I'd love to see universities engaging students and staff in the conversation about what's important to them about the future of HE, and promoting dialogue with communities around the valuable role that institutions play. If we see the traffic as two-way between institutions and the Accord, we miss the opportunity for the rich dialogue with others who matter.

Ensure that marginal ideas are raised. There are well-funded and well-organised lobby groups in the HE sector which have had a lot of time to hone their skills in policy influence. They will be coordinated in their approach to the Accord and make compelling arguments. It's vital that other voices are heard too, and that there is opportunity to explore ideas from different angles. It may be that the lobby groups are right, but their role is to speak for part of the sector, not the whole. This is why it's important for more voices to engage in the process, to offer solutions and not just leave it to vested interests.

The Accord process will run its course, but there is an opportunity to do more, to add more value to the activity by using the structure of the review to support a dialogue about the place of HE in society. I have many conversations which surface a concern about universities' social licence to operate. The sector shouldn't wait for the outcomes of a review which may or may not have any impact. It is incumbent on leaders across the sector to use the process as a means to broader ends.

Universities should use the full breadth of their capabilities to shape the sector for the better, and in doing so, educate their stakeholders about the value and potential of HE. The opportunity in universities' autonomy comes from the acceptance of the constraints provided by the system, recognition that there is a misalignment of incentives for delivering the best outcomes for beneficiaries, and using agency to shape conditions for the better.

Implications for governance and leadership

Leaders in HE must maintain a relentless focus on the benefits which their universities provide. They need to optimise performance for the greatest possible benefit. However, striking the right balance between short-term outcomes and long-term benefits is a tightrope which leaders must walk. Universities are not immune to the pressure of immediate results, yet their real value lies in their long-lasting contributions to knowledge and societal development. Leaders must ensure that they cultivate cultures which value enduring impact over transient success. Universities, at their best, are open, inclusive, ambitious environments that foster intellectual growth and societal advancement. Yet, the prevailing incentives and conditions can often undermine these positive cultures. Therefore, leaders must play a pivotal role in upholding and nurturing a positive culture, despite these challenges. And leaders are not merely operators within the university system; they should also be drivers of its evolution. With their rich experience and intricate understanding of the sector, leaders have a crucial role in shaping policy that can enhance the HE landscape.

Good governance of our universities is also essential to positive outcomes for stakeholders. Boards, too, play a pivotal role in defining the trajectory of their universities. They must champion their institutions, articulating the university's contributions to society and advocating for its recognition and support. They also need to strike the delicate balance between serving the interests of individuals and those of society. Universities must cater to the needs of their students and staff, but they also bear the responsibility to advance the public good. The strategies and approaches which governing bodies sign off, monitor, and review must continue to pursue both short-term outcomes and long-term benefits. And all with financial sustainability in mind. This means having proper accountability for institutional leaders providing support as well as challenge.

Leading the contemporary university – and the future one – is a difficult task of trade-offs with the need to pursue benefits across the many dimensions of institutional activity and seek outcomes across different temporal horizons. It is only with clarity on how universities create value for individuals and communities that the task of leadership can be achieved. And it is only through understanding and exploration of the way policies and incentives play out within the university that leaders can understand how best to use the opportunities which come from autonomy, both to shape their institutions and advocate for change in the sector.

What would be different in the future university?

- Universities are clear about how their quasi-autonomy enables them to operate with some freedoms. This clarity supports effective decision making and empowers universities to stay true to delivering their mission.
- No university is complacent about its position in society. There is a positive and expansive narrative shared widely about the role and purpose of universities. Universities recognise their pasts but focus effort on celebrating the here and now, and painting optimistic visions of the future.
- The focus on mission and outcomes changes university incentives such that they aim to create maximum benefit for each individual member of their community, as well as in aggregate. Universities forego some income where delivery of education would not benefit students.
- University leaders are the best of the best. Leaders combine academic expertise with the experience and judgement necessary for the complexities of the future university, and they recognise that leading a university is a team sport.

**

HE provides significant benefit to individuals, and to wider society. While HE institutions continue to operate with the protections of oversight and governance for the reasonable use of public and private money, they should be nurtured for the good of society. There is enormous value in the continued existence of institutions with the triple-helix mission. They provide convening spaces; are part of social infrastructure, like civil defence or natural disaster situations; and they offer cultural engagement activities that might be unsustainable if they were standalone organisations. Universities should not be ashamed about the benefits which they create for individuals, and for society collectively, and it may be advantageous to explain the differences between these goals and how the various functions of universities speak to them.

Given the unusual position of universities in a liminal space between public and private, institutions should take advantage of where they sit to take the best of both worlds. And they should do this selectively and critically. The answer for the imaginative future of the university cannot simply be 'behave like a private business' or 'focus exclusively on public benefit'. The marketised systems provides for this, but too much of the discourse seeks to complain about the constraints that it provides, with too little optimism about the freedoms that it also offers.

Make universities joyful[15]

Universities survive because people want to work in them and students want to study at them. The marketised HE systems have paid too little attention to staff wellbeing as the essential underpinning for positive outcomes. There is a need to rebalance the emphasis in the university away from performance indicators, which focus too much on short-term returns and too little on the long-term benefits that come from universities being places where people can do their best work. This chapter engages with the threats to joy in contemporary HE institutions to make the case that this is indeed a problem worth solving.

Innovation for its own sake is not enough: there needs to be a potential solution, and one which can make a material benefit to the sector through change at the institutional level. Regulated HE systems are capable of being more joyful places. It is reasonable to seek innovations which change the operating and environmental conditions for institutions, but they will likely to take longer to implement, and they may never happen at all if the levers for change exist beyond the sector. If we focus on identification of the problem and the solutions within the purview of the institution, then we can empower the leaders of those institutions to act.

We cannot wait for a joyful HE system to be bestowed upon us. We need to increase the levels of joy within contemporary HE, linking longer-term strategy making and incentives with tactical actions which demonstrate the commitment to greater joy. These solutions must be human-centred, with a focus on how

---

15 This chapter is an adapted version of the essay shortlisted for the Dr Jonathan Nicholls Essay Prize 2023 organised by the UK's Association of Heads of University Administration.

enabling more joyful places of learning and work contributes to the mission for HE. And in this work there must be an emphasis on equity: there is no point in joy just for some; we must have the conditions and potential for everyone to experience joy.

Joy is worth fighting for

At the height of the Global Financial Crisis, French President Nicholas Sarkozy asked Professors Joseph Stiglitz, Amartya Sen, and Jean-Paul Fitoussi to investigate ways to measure economic performance. Their report proposed a greater focus on wellbeing alongside production, and on how equitably consumption is distributed.[16] This report hardly marked the death of Gross Domestic Product as the central measure of a country's economic activity, but it opened up the potential of richer measures of success. The idea resonated with British Prime Minister David Cameron who, in 2010, introduced new measures for national wellbeing.[17] Data from the UK's Office for National Statistics show that happiness ratings are heading back up, after a significant dip in the COVID pandemic, but that they have yet to return to previous highs.[18] It is time for the HE sector to reflect on whether its ambitions, and its measures of success, have become too focussed on instrumental outcomes, with too little attention paid to the affective experience of staff and students.

Joy might sound like too wishy-washy a concept for some. I think of joy as taking pleasure beyond mere satisfaction. Happiness also fails to capture the richness of the emotion. Joy is a state deep in one's body where the endorphins flow, and in the mind where the neurons fire. This is not what one expects of management speak. The case for joy lies in the vocation – the drive to work for something greater than one's own personal reward – which motivates many, perhaps most, people in HE. In my experience, this vocation is present whether colleagues have a professional role, an academic one, or a hybrid position. Joy is also defined by its absence, and it is arguable that the contemporary university

....

16   J E Stiglitz, A Sen, and J-P Fitoussi, 'Report by the Commission on the Measurement of Economic Performance and Social Progress', 2009. Available from: ec.europa.eu/eurostat/documents/8131721/8131772/Stiglitz-Sen-Fitoussi-Commission-report.pdf.

17   D Cameron, PM speech on wellbeing, 25 November 2010. Available from: www.gov.uk/government/speeches/pm-speech-on-wellbeing.

18   Office for National Statistics, 'Measures of National Well-Being Dashboard: Quality of Life in the UK', 11 November 2022. Available from: www.ons.gov.uk/peoplepopulationandcommunity/wellbeing/articles/measuresofnationalwellbeingdashboardqualityoflifeintheuk/2022-08-12.

is a place which has reduced joy or, in some cases, eliminated it. For HE to be a sector which attracts people, provides the conditions in which they can flourish, and encourages them to stay and contribute for as long as appropriate, more attention needs to be paid to professional joy. My argument is for a systemic joy, for the conditions in which everyone who works for, or studies in, an HE institution is likely to find joy in their interactions.

The pursuit of joy should also be consistent with well-run institutions which respond to the needs of their communities. One model for thinking about the intersecting motivations which support the academic endeavour is Alice Lam's model of puzzle, ribbon, and gold.[19] This psychological approach, applied to what motivates researchers to engage in commercialisation, has the potential for broader application, as it highlights the multiplicity of motivations within one person. It is a model likely to resonate with those across the sector who recognise the motivational qualities of solving problems (puzzle), recognition of that work (ribbon), and financial reward (gold). This model reflects the attractive qualities of intellectual stimulation which are peculiar to HE institutions. It is because of the intersecting motivations for working in HE that the sector would benefit from conceptions of personal achievement – in my terms, joy – which reflect the distinctive context. While we can draw on the principles of measuring happiness, particularly the emphasis on the equitable distribution of wellbeing, there is a case for recognising the unique context of HE and developing an HE-tailored approach to creating joyful environments for work and study.

The threats to joy

I have followed the #leavingacademia discourse with interest. There are people – perhaps only a small number, but vocal – who have shared their experiences of the transition away from academic careers around the world. There are good reasons for their choices. For many in academic careers, the precarious nature of post-doctoral positions is unsustainable. Workloads and expectations are high. The contemporary academic must produce a steady stream of high quality 'output' while also seeking impact, satisfying students' needs and wants, contributing to their institutions and their fields, having a public and social media presence, and generating income to sustain their livelihood. These demands are not all new, but there is increasing pressure in each area, and additional layers of scrutiny of

....
19 A Lam, 'What motivates academic scientists to engage in research commercialization: "Gold," "ribbon" or "puzzle"?', *Research Policy* 40:10, 2011, 1354–1368.

performance. We also know that these burdens are unequal, depending on where any individual is in their career, by institution, and their personal characteristics. Academic life can be hard, and it's not fair.

It isn't simply academic careers which are challenging. The pandemic has had major negative impacts for individual health and for society. COVID is just one factor which posed a challenge to universities' funding, with borders closed to international students and new resources required to support online learning. In the context of constrained resources, many HE providers have had to become more efficient. Cuts often mean that the remaining staff must do more with less. There is always some efficiency to be gained, but the overall effect is to make working in universities and other HE institutions harder. The commercial and consumer pressures within HE are pervasive, and the implications are felt widely. If we add to this a mental health crisis among students and staff, sexual violence, industrial disputes, media and political criticism, and the wider context of cost of living, global conflict, and the existential threat of climate disaster, there is a lot to worry about. Many of these factors affect all areas of society, but rather than accept these conditions, there is an imperative for HE to find solutions (or mitigations, at least) which fit the sector's context.

There is regular complaint that the marketised HE system, particularly that imposed on the English sector by the *Higher Education and Research Act 2017*, is the cause of the sector's woes. There are longstanding issues in the sector which long pre-date the creation of the Office for Students, like securing the sustainability of pension schemes. While the problems of marketisation have been explored extensively, it is often undervalued that within this quasi-market is a significant opportunity for institutional differentiation. The scope of institutional autonomy allows the sector's leaders to set and deliver on nuanced strategies which achieve the missions of HE in ways which are right for their institutions. It is this freedom of action, within the regulated environment, which provides the space to assert new and different ways of working, such as seeking greater joy. Leaders have the power to address the threats to joy.

Institutions can be more joyful places

During the pandemic, some universities tried, in good faith, to support staff wellbeing through extra leave and tokens of thanks. Some of these were derided as cynical tokens which failed to grasp the true extent of the challenges facing colleagues. This reaction seems entirely fair, given that those same institutions were laying off staff in significant numbers. But, more interestingly, it shows how large the gap is between institutional leaders' ambition to make things better, if only in comparatively small ways, and staff perceptions of leadership. For HE institutions to be successful, this is a gap which must be bridged. HE institutions which are respectful and supportive environments should also be places of creativity and exploration where people want to make their careers. Joyful workplaces should also be places of joy in learning capable of supporting students to achieve joyful lives through the outcomes that they seek from education.

A focus on joy should not be seen as a 'soft' option for running an institution. There should be no excuses which prevent tackling bullying or other negative behaviours. Pursuit of one person's joy should not impinge on others' happiness. This is perhaps the most crucial part of the mindset shift in seeking joyful HE institutions: joy must contribute to the mission. The 'employee value proposition' will be enriched as the institution gains a reputation as a joyful place, great staff and students are attracted and stay, and the institution will be a place of great outcomes as a result. This is a deep commitment to a positive environment, and outcomes which cannot be achieved with cynicism. The authenticity of the commitment will need to shine through. If it does, and my hypothesis holds, there will be many people better off for the transition.

Making the joyful university

To reshape HE institutions towards joy, we need radical change. The shift should be worth it, and it is within the gift of institutions to effect the necessary change. But that change will be hard, and it will be difficult to make it stick. The solutions I propose start with that which is most important for long-term success but which will unlikely show results in the short term. Changing cultures through language and actions will take time, and it will be necessary to have some 'quick wins' to demonstrate the seriousness of the commitment and deliver some tangible outcomes.

1. **Make joy a foundational and pervasive part of institutional strategy**
   While university strategies are regularly derided as being too similar, too obvious, or too vague, they are the assertion of the institutional goals and they are read. Strategies are signed off by governing bodies and circulated widely to communicate to colleagues, and the outside world, what the university stands for and what it aims to achieve. All strategies need to speak to the mission of

HE institutions to promote research, education, and engagement, but they do so in the unique and specific context of each provider. The language of joy should pervade strategies by speaking to the personal impact of the overall institutional policy settings and decisions. We do not need a separate 'pillar' to promote joy, but we need language – and associated actions – which place joy within each element of the strategy.

A commitment among the senior leaders to systemic joy is the foundation of a positive change. Some time ago, I was part of a discussion with senior leaders in a university about proposed pension changes. The majority of the time was spent discussing senior academics' own personal – and very generous – pension arrangements, rather than the substantive question of how the other ninety-nine per cent might be affected. Joy will only come from realising the hard truth that access to joy is inequitably distributed within the institution. Older colleagues are more likely to have secured security of their professional standing, more generous pensions, and houses owned outright. More senior jobs pay more, and they also offer greater flexibility. For joy to be lived out for everyone, there needs to be a heartfelt commitment to understanding the realities of life on the frontline, be that in teaching or the tearoom, research, or registry.

We do not need a Chief Joy Officer. Senior leaders need to be mandated to seek joy within their portfolios as a leadership approach which they cascade through the organisation. The actions which leaders take, and the changes that they need to make, will vary widely, based on the current state and the scope for change. This variety should be embraced as experimentation from which other parts of the institution can learn. And in adopting approaches which promote joy, leaders will need to recognise that there are trade-offs. It cannot be a short-term change but a material shift in approach which means sticking consistently to the principles even in the face of difficulty or opposition.

Ultimately, the strategy document, in itself, changes nothing. It is the actions associated with the document which will make meaningful change to the lives of staff and students. The change must start somewhere, and that place should be at the 'top'.

2. **Collaborate to build a common language for joy within the institution**
I've proposed starting with institutional strategy, because if the senior team at the institution fails to get behind the need for joy, the plan will go nowhere. Passive resistance is a common phenomenon, particularly in universities, and

trying to make a bottom-up movement for change is easily blocked.[20] However, this strategy approach needs to be complemented by an active process for engaging staff about the opportunities for joy in their respective roles, how that might be described, and how to live out that joy.

Joy is deeply personal. It is not something which the institution can simply hand out. Nor will words ever be enough to give confidence that the institution is systemically a joyful place. The methods for understanding the opportunities for joy should be collaborative and engaging. The principles of human-centred design are very useful here: start with personal experiences and build from there. Not everyone will want to engage, and those who do will have a range of preferences for approach. HE institutions are large, complex, and diverse. What matters in one part of the institution, or for one subset of the community, may not be relevant for another. It is only by engaging widely that we understand the nuances and can therefore build appropriate responses.[21]

The outcomes of the engagement process, which should be ongoing and embedded in staff consultation approaches, should be statements about what joy can, and should, mean at the institution. This may include guidance on how to create a more joyful place for work and learning. Colleagues may benefit from that guidance which shows the actions which they can take to support a joyful working environment. The articulation of joy should also be reflected in staff recruitment and performance assessment, and should pervade institutional policies so that every part provides a 'nudge' to create a better and more inclusive environment. Embedding a cycle of understanding the level, and distribution, of joy within the institution, followed by the proportionate actions which promote joy, is vital to achieve transformation.

3. **Remove barriers to joy**

Long-term approaches to promote joy are essential if cultural change is to be achieved. However, staff may, reasonably, be sceptical about the motivations

---

20 If you want to test that idea, ask any students' union officer about the difference when campaigning for something which senior members of a university think is important and something they disagree with, or don't care about.

21 In the context of systemic and institutional racism, the pursuit of joy may sound like a cruel joke. It is not meant to be patronising, or to diminish the real gap that exists between the experiences of staff – particularly people of colour – and an acceptable state. I recognise that a joyful state is a privilege, and one which should be extended to everyone, regardless of their personal characteristics or status within the institution.

and ambitions for a new, joyful approach. It is possible, even likely, to be seen as a fad. Engagement approaches only give confidence that change is possible when they manifest in experiences. For an institution to take on this approach, it must find some ways to demonstrate a commitment to removing as many barriers to joy in the short term, before it sees the fruits of strategic change. Initiatives will likely have cost implications, with payoffs only later, as the institution benefits from being a more desirable and effective place to work and study. Focussing any additional investment on the lowest-earning staff would have the greatest proportionate impact on their lives and give benefits to larger numbers.

Examples of possible actions include:

1. **Double-down on celebrating success.** Institutions typically have staff awards and other recognition points across the year: these are important 'ribbon' opportunities and are a vital component of the motivational model. Ensure that these are made regular occurrences, and that all staff have the opportunity for recognition. Celebrating collective achievements may be even more impactful than individual performance and promote a sense of common purpose.
2. **Teach everyone how to give empathetic feedback.** Remind everyone what is expected in terms of behaviour to create inclusive environments. Ensure that senior leaders model institutional values. Empower colleagues to challenge when standards fall short of what is expected, and support them to challenge those in more senior positions. Remind students and staff that everyone is fallible, and that everyone can learn from feedback on their actions.
3. **Tackle bullies.** Become a place where bullying and harassment are not tolerated, and empower leaders and managers to address situations where people display joy-sapping behaviours. As staff see that negative behaviours are no longer tolerated, their confidence will grow that the institution takes their wellbeing seriously.
4. **Make available the full resources of the institution to staff in need.** Ensure that all staff are aware of support available for their personal circumstances in times of crisis or for ongoing support. If there are gaps in provision, or evidence that some groups take up less help than expected, investigate to ensure that the right level of support is getting to those who need it.

5. **Improve the pay and conditions of the lowest earners** by ensuring – as an absolute minimum – that the institution pays a genuine living wage appropriate to its location, and that it has contracts which provide staff with the right amount and level of work.[22]

The actions which institutions take will necessarily reflect their local context and circumstances. In a resource-constrained environment, it may be hard to make the case for further investments in pursuit of systemic joy. I suspect that institutions will find that there are ways of getting better 'for free'; that is, doing the same sort of activities but working in ways which promote joy. I have proposed some low-cost interventions which will demonstrate a good faith commitment to promoting a joyful environment. If the theory holds, however, there should also be good-value, larger investments which improve the conditions and reputation of the institution and deliver significant return on investment. It may be a gamble to focus effort beyond traditional measures, but if we get more joy along the way, then that is a risk worth taking.

What would be different in the future university?

- University leaders and governing bodies put joy on their agendas. In addition to standard performance measures, universities find ways to understand and articulate what it means to be joyful places of work. Measuring how equitably joy is distributed is a foundation for more inclusive universities.
- The universities which enable joyful work attract the best talent and enable them to flourish. Reputations are built on a broad conception of performance, including how all staff are treated, fuelling virtuous cycles of increasingly joyful universities.
- Universities are known as fair, humane, and respectful places of work. Staff are attracted from other sectors to work in universities because it is, all round, a better place to be.
- Universities are places of safety, enabling intellectual and professional endeavours to be pursued without fear. Joy-sapping behaviours are challenged and resolved.

---

22   Jonathan Grant wrote for Wonkhe in January 2023 that 'two-thirds of universities do not pay a real living wage, and a quarter of those that claim to be civic do not pay a real or voluntary living wage'. See: wonkhe.com/blogs/are-universities-still-civic-washing.

***

There is a need for greater joy in HE. The pursuit of joy, systemically and ongoing, will reap benefits which better deliver against the mission of HE institutions for education, research, and social impact. But we need to make joy tangible to avoid it being a vacuous platitude. It must be consistent and heartfelt, not cynical. Collaborative and human-centred approaches are needed to ensure that joy is achieved authentically in ways which make a genuine positive difference to the lives of staff and students. Joy must be equitable. It is currently unevenly distributed, and we need to understand how joy is a privilege which should be extended to everyone. This approach will support a positive impact for the wider communities served by HE institutions driving benefits beyond traditional measures of output. Given the challenges facing institutions, and the wider world, this has to be worth a try.

Celebrate some inefficiency

Universities cannot just pursue efficient operation as this threatens the environment for knowledge creation and sharing. For universities to be places of joyful work, and for the achievement of their purposes, they need to be well run. Money makes the world go round, and universities aren't exempt from the cold hard reality of the need to conserve every dollar or pound. This chapter first makes the case that universities have to be run in pursuit of inefficiency. They need the space and flexibility to take risks, to be brave in their decisions, and for things to go wrong. But they get that room for inefficiency in the pursuit of their purposes only if they are efficient in how they run as organisations. The future university must be able to diversify its income streams, including working with partners; use its intellectual and technological tools for continuous improvement; and evaluate critically how to achieve the appropriate scale.

Make the case for inefficiency

On one interpretation of a university's performance, a large financial surplus at the end of the year looks great. That means there's more money in the rainy-day fund, more capital to invest into the latest shiny new building project, less costly debt, and the security that comes from knowing that the lights will be kept on and bills will be paid long into the future. But, simultaneously, a large surplus represents failure. That is the failure to invest this year for the needs of the students and staff we have now. It is the failure to ensure that every current opportunity has been maximised, traded for a far-off potential benefit. We can't have it both ways: universities need to build their long-term resilience to allow for shocks and major investments, and they need to invest for today.

Often, the nuance of university finance gets lost in the debate on surpluses and deficits, or in a focus on executive remuneration. These are important, but they miss the essential economics of the university, which is not the pursuit of efficiency. We are not trying to drive all costs to their absolute minima. Some costs, yes, but the mission drive of the university is actually to spend as much as possible delivering education, research, and social impact. It is entirely consistent with the marketised system and neoliberal university that we benchmark every inch of university performance and try to squeeze out the most productivity, even where we know that we don't have the measures to really judge performance. We're not making widgets but providing places of learning and creativity and impact. I tried to make this case for the Committee for Economic Development of Australia[23] in the context of the Universities Accord:

> *Missing in the debate about the Universities Accord is the case for the in-built inefficiency in higher education. There is a reason that universities exist with combined missions of education, research, and engagement. At their best, these work together to deliver a broad range of positive outcomes for students, the economy, and communities. Funding these institutions with some flexibility requires a level of trust which is not the typical framing of Australian public policy.*
>
> *Universities need to support students' ability to get jobs, and to be effective in those jobs. But they also need to enable students to think expansively and critically about what they might want to do, and where and how to do it. Higher education would be much less effective if it were to be reduced to the training-package model of vocational education. Equally, researchers need the time and space (and colleagues and equipment) to explore ideas with creativity. Economic benefits will come, but in time.*
>
> *The idea of a higher education system with in-built inefficiency isn't just an indulgence. Creating a system that allows students and staff to explore ideas is grounded in the pursuit of competitive advantage. In the global*

---

23 See the full blog post, 'Universities Accord could set direction for the next generation', at https://www.ceda.com.au/NewsAndResources/Opinion/Education/Universities-Accord-could-set-direction-for-the-ne.

context, Australian higher education needs to focus more on being the destination for global talent. We want brilliant people building their careers and doing their best work in Australia.

We already have a great quality of life, good salaries by international standards, and reputed universities. We don't, however, have the culture and incentives to attract the very top academics. Artificial intelligence is great for many things, but it has not yet replaced researchers as creators of new knowledge, nor teachers as empathic communicators and sources of inspiration. There is a tendency in policy reviews to think too narrowly about the mechanisms of change. For the Accord to succeed, it should set out principles by which the sector should function for the next generation.

Those principles should support achieving short-term positive impacts for students and other stakeholders, such as making it easier for universities to collaborate with businesses and industry associations. Those principles should also express broader ambitions for a world-leading system of higher education. Australia has enormously successful universities. We would all be richer if the Universities Accord builds on the success in the system to allow educators and researchers freedom to pursue longer-term goals. Some inefficiency may seem a hard concept to support, not least when government finances are tight. But for a successful higher education sector fit to serve the next generation, some thoughtful inefficiency is what we need.

When asking for a greater share of taxpayer funding – competing against all the other priorities – it is probably foolish to make a case on the basis of inefficiency. But we need universities to think in this way, and to articulate where and how that in-built inefficiency is good for the long-term health of the sector as a whole, and for humanity. It is only through pursuit of efficiency in the right areas and the development of well-run right-sized institutions which use their capabilities for self-improvement that the licence for inefficiency will be granted.

Diversify your income streams

Universities need money if they are going to deliver on their purposes. While the core of a university's revenue will come from its education offer (both tuition and aligned services for students like accommodation), and from externally-funded research, institutions also need to pursue other streams to give them flexibility, and to cover the costs of their thoughtful inefficiency.

One of the difficult parts of the conversations in universities about diversifying income streams in any meaningful way is that ancillary streams take a long time to mature and make meaningful impacts on the finances. For many universities, the marginal return of gaining a few more international students will outstrip a side project. But, thinking for the long-term health of the institution, universities need to expand how they generate the revenue for reinvestment in the mission. Few universities in the UK or Australia generate substantial revenue from philanthropy, when compared to their tuition turnover, but they should continue to pursue this area. Similarly, universities need to stimulate further research commercialisation with the aim of some return, even if the likelihood of significant sums is low. Summer schools and conference centres provide some universities with a few million each year, 'sweating the assets' of the institution for an all-year-round return. The whole point of diversifying income streams is to find the marginal additional dollar or pound which gives the university freedom to invest without any constraints from a funding body. After the costs of generating that income have been accounted for, this is the money with fewest constraints on its application.

Where universities could look to expand further is in services for the HE sector. There are some notable examples where individual universities, such as the University of Warwick's ownership of job site jobs.ac.uk, or groups, as in Australian universities' sometime ownership of international student recruitment channel IDP Education, operate activities which benefit the sector and for which the benefit is captured by the sector. There are good reasons to see expansion in sector-facing products and services rather than investment in any other area; universities understand the problems that they face and, therefore, the potential solutions, better than they do the challenges in other sectors. This provides an advantage in the competitive landscape. It can also be difficult to sell services to universities, but sector-owned services are likely to be seen more favourably and thereby reduce the cost of sale when compared to fully private options. There is, of course, the risk of mission drift, were a university to become simply another investor or builder of businesses. Keeping it in the sector makes sense commercially, and is also aligned to mission.

There are different models for developing sector businesses. These might be the traditional wholly-owned subsidiaries, like many university presses, or joint ventures with private businesses, like some online programme management companies. Co-investment with the private sector could bring additional capital and different capabilities which might be difficult to have, or recruit for, in the university. Sharing of the risks of a start-up also means sharing the rewards, but it may be commercially advantageous to 'go big'. Every university could find its niche service which could solve problems for the sector while generating and capturing the benefits, or groups of universities could work together to reduce the up-front barriers to developing a commercial proposition and to share in the benefits. Universities should seek actively to build their commercial side projects to establish the businesses which will grow over time to provide meaningful revenue to the university. Capturing the benefits within the sector also means not being beholden to private companies like university-ranking providers or the publishing giants.

Build the self-optimising university

I floated the idea of the self-optimising university at an event with deputy vice-chancellors for education. One of them immediately responded, 'Don't you know how hard it is to get academics to help the university?' It has always baffled me, and I know that I am not alone, that universities fail to use the capabilities that they have within the institution to run better. I realise that it is hard to get help, particularly from academics, because the current incentive structures militate against working on institutional matters, which are a diversion from the core individual imperative of doing impactful research. But I think that we can change the incentives, or at least create new roles and opportunities which enable a university to unlock the potential of its intellectual capabilities to make every part of what it does, and how it's done, work better every day.

The concept of the learning organisation[24] is a highly attractive and now long-standing one. Universities should be places in which learning takes place not just for students, nor just in pushing the frontiers of research; they should, as corporate entities, also be capable of learning. I would like to see universities go beyond being learning organisations and use the capabilities of institutional research, of experimentation, to optimise everything they do. From the ways that people move around campus to engaging with online learning to managing

---

24 See Diana Laurillard, 'A conversational framework for individual learning applied to the "learning organisation" and the "learning society"', *Systems Research and Behavioural Science*, 1999, 16, 113–122.

bad debt and ensuring good quality feedback to students, everything can be improved. And, of course, universities should use the tools that they have available through experimental design, data gathering and analysis, and ethics and governance to make every dimension of the university work better. Better may come in different ways, from cost saving to improving quality or system resilience. And it is now with increasingly cheap and sophisticated AI that we can more easily deploy tools for optimisation. The point is that the university should move from piecemeal self-interrogation and improvement to large-scale and continuous iteration and refinement.

I believe strongly that a small number of universities will alight on this approach as the answer to their internal challenges and use this capability to move away from the others. The self-optimising university will be able to grow at much faster rates than other universities because it understands the implications of growth better and can minimise the 'growing pains' on staff, students, and the physical and virtual estates. This university will achieve better staff and student satisfaction, know how to price its services to maximise return, and generate the largest possible surpluses for reinvestment, which will make it a research powerhouse. The self-optimising university can be the place where the full mission is delivered, where education, research, and social impact each achieve the highest levels of excellence, not one diminished for the others to succeed. The advent of new AI tools offering rapid productivity gains will further accelerate the differentiation of performance: those which adopt these approaches will get better, faster, and leave others in their wake. The universities which get here first will also capture more value for themselves if they then help others to build the capabilities, selling the valuable services and insights to others in the sector.

Universities are uniquely placed to become self-optimising institutions. It will take new people and systems to make it happen, but universities should be able to find both, because they offer the environments in which this approach can succeed. Few universities will pursue the route of self-optimisation, but those which do, which invest in the tools and resources to bring this to life, will be the institutions that succeed in the long term. They will be able to see the threats and opportunities and seize them before others. They will provide greater value through their education, and they will have more impactful research. And it is the understanding that the university, as a next-level learning organisation, should capitalise on its rare capabilities that will make this happen.

Right-size the university

Universities are the product of their histories, of demographics and locations. In general, they try to grow to have a greater impact, and they follow the imperative of the marketised system to compete for students. More students equals more success. But there is a different way to look at the question of what right-sizing the university is, and whether it's time to ask whether the missions of the institution can be better served through different structures and collaborations. Mergers between institutions are, unsurprisingly, often favoured by consultants who see both the corporate opportunities for what the post-merger institution might do and the commercial opportunity in helping the process to happen. But aside from this external pressure for institutions to change their form, there are important questions that university leaders and governing bodies should ask about their institutional futures; for example:

- Can distinctive missions, such as serving specific communities, be better achieved through collaboration?
- How do our current incentives and biases support, or prevent, us from thinking creatively about the best future for the institution?
- Should we seek to build education groups across levels, including schools or vocational provision, to complement HE or look for cross-HE partners?

Universities looking to enhance their operational efficiency often encounter a crossroads: should they consider merging with other institutions, or focus on strengthening their individual capabilities? It's worth exploring the potential paths in both directions to appreciate their relative merits and limitations. Let's take a scenario where several universities in a densely populated and well-served metropolitan area decide to merge. These universities, each located strategically across the region, independently serve a large number of students and generate significant financial turnover. However, on their own, they might struggle to secure the investment needed for innovations in education, research, or capital infrastructural projects due to the high costs associated with such a densely populated area.

A merger in this scenario could offer substantial benefits, such as financial resilience through combined resources, lower costs of education design and delivery through shared portfolios, and ensuring minimum cohort viability by pooling student populations. Moreover, a merged institution could have more influence in policy debates and a stronger international reputation. Such a consolidation would require brave leadership willing to forego individual institutional identities for a greater collective purpose. There might be substantial resistance, and success would rely on careful planning and persuasive negotiation. Yet, the potential advantages make such an endeavour worth considering.

However, a merger isn't the right solution for every situation. Consider another scenario where multiple universities, each occupying a distinct market position and brand identity, contemplate merging. Here, the distinct identity and specialisation of each university might outweigh the perceived benefits of a merger. For instance, one institution might be a traditional, research-intensive university; another could focus on teaching and vocational education; the third might excel in applied research and industry engagement. A merger could potentially dilute these unique identities. Instead of enhancing the overall reputation, a merger might result in negative perceptions. One argument favouring the merger could be to attain a larger scale and increase their global ranking. However, this approach appears to outsource the judgement of institutional success to third-party ranking bodies. What's the alternative? Instead of a merger, a more fruitful approach could be to focus on strengthening each university's unique capabilities. A combination of strategies could be designed to enhance the strengths of each university, encouraging high-quality research and fostering a positive reputation.

Achieving operational efficiency in universities requires a nuanced understanding of each institution's specific context, strengths, and challenges. A one-size-fits-all approach isn't likely to work. Whether through strategic mergers or individual growth strategies, universities must be ready to innovate and adapt to serve their students effectively, contribute to knowledge, and maintain financial and operational sustainability.

What would be different in the future university?

- There is a widespread understanding among policymakers, the public, and within institutions that universities need to balance operational efficiency with investment inefficiency to ensure that they achieve the triple helix of their mission. The social contract is understood and well-articulated.
- Entrepreneurial mindsets enable universities to capture more of the value of their activities for the good of institutions and the sector. Individually and collectively, universities find ways to generate surpluses and reduce costs for reinvestment in their missions.

- Universities are true learning organisations using the intellectual and technical capabilities for self-optimisation. They use experimental techniques every day to test and learn for continual improvement.
- University leaders and governing bodies consistently ask whether their current institutional form is the best way to deliver on their mission of their institution. There is reward and recognition where difficult decisions are made, such as closing an institution, for the greater good of the sector and to achieve better outcomes for stakeholders.

***

Universities need to be places of inefficiency. But that scope inefficiency is earned through an entrepreneurial approach that creates the surplus for reinvestment which is nice to have, but not essential. Every institution also needs to target ongoing improvement through pursuit of self-optimisation built on the expertise and tools – with the appropriate ethics and governance – using the institution's intellectual and technical assets. And while these are the day-to-day imperatives, universities must also ask whether their missions can be better delivered through mergers or other collaborations. These are difficult questions which can only be answered truthfully if leaders hold firm to delivering on their missions and creating value for graduates and communities at large.

Treat education as your product

A university education should be expansive, exciting, enriching, and challenging. It should prepare students for careers and not just jobs. Degrees offer opportunities in learning how to learn which prepare graduates to have enriching lifelong intellectual growth. Education is vital to the university mission and that education should be extended widely and equitably to ensure that all with the capacity to benefit can enjoy its fruits. But it also needs to be delivered efficiently for universities to survive.

Academic freedom is a fundamental quality of what makes universities special. But that freedom should be exercised in research, in creative and expansive intellectual inquiry. In teaching, there should be freedom in how education is delivered to ensure that the work of the educator is interesting and engaging. Individual academic freedom, however, can no longer extend to that which is taught; we need to focus on students' needs and the outcomes they are pursuing. The course portfolio is an institutional decision which requires thoughtful planning and efficient execution. Education is the way in which universities create value for students, and it is only through understanding it as a product, and organising the university to deliver that product well, that HE institutions will generate the surpluses they need for investment in their research and social impact missions.

The case for product strategy

The future of learning and teaching in universities calls for an innovative product approach, where the primary focus is not merely on the educational process but on the desired outcome and the overall learning experience. Implementing this approach necessitates a series of steps, some of which may present challenges for universities, but which, ultimately, can lead to transformative changes in HE. The first step in the product approach is to define clearly the outcomes and assessment measures. This serves as the blueprint for design and implementation. Outcomes should be related to real-world skills and competencies, reflecting the requirements of employers and societal needs. Assessment measures should focus on authentic demonstrations of learning, rather than merely regurgitating information.

To operationalise the product approach, we need to conceptualise an educational product cycle. This begins with understanding learners' needs, followed by the curriculum design, education delivery, and assessment of learning outcomes. The cycle ends with the review and improvement of the product, based on feedback from learners and the performance of graduates in the job market. This approach ensures that nothing is missing and that the education provided remains relevant and impactful. Communicating product features is also an essential part of this approach. Prospective students should understand not only what they will learn but also what they will be able to do with their education. This requires clear, transparent communication about learning outcomes, career prospects, and the broader learning experience.

While transitioning to this model, universities may face hard truths, such as the existence of poor-value courses, unmet needs, and negative student experiences. They may find that their settings so far have led to over-servicing students, normalising courses with greater learning volumes than students need. A focus on the benefit to students should protect them from this perverse incentive even if it means institutions foregoing some income that they might otherwise have gained. These issues can serve as a wake-up call and an impetus for change. It's essential to learn from these pitfalls and draw inspiration from successful examples elsewhere. In the product approach, universities act as platforms which provide the infrastructure for learning. They make the necessary investments and, in turn, should expect a return on investment. The return comes in the form of graduates who succeed in their careers, enhance the university's reputation, and contribute to society.

The product approach goes beyond the core educational offer. It encompasses the broader learning experience, including extracurricular activities, personal development opportunities, and community engagement. However, it's essential to recognise that different students value different aspects of the experience.

There is a delicate balance between product development as standardisation and the flexibility and personalisation required to ensure that each student can have a positive experience and find their own joy in the journey of being and becoming as a learner. This is all the more reason for a product approach; if we are to have mass HE, we need first to identify what benefits groups most, and then use technologies with humans to provide students with tailored experiences. We must reject the amateur approach to education and professionalise to create more benefits more consistently.

What if we need resources to do things differently? It is entirely possible that transitioning to a product approach will create costs for universities, but it is through the full realisation of this approach, not least the more granular understanding of institutional costs, which will release financial surpluses. In the short term, however, there are ways to find the money to support transition. First, the pandemic showed us some physical infrastructure might be unnecessary. This can potentially free up capital for investment in teaching and learning. Secondly, borrowing is an option for many universities, given that lenders see the long-term benefits of investing in quality education. A product-focussed business plan may be compelling to many lenders which see the potential gains in new approaches. Lastly, co-investment models work where universities partner with companies to develop and deliver online programmes, sharing the costs and benefits.

What if staff object to doing things differently? Industrial relations in HE typically lead to incremental changes in conditions. The proposals here are more radical than the current scope for change and will therefore take time or significant incentives to be achieved, and most likely both. Future teaching-focussed jobs need not to be seen as inferior either to research careers or to a more traditional combined research and teaching role. Their benefits will need to be sold to colleagues. A focus on the positive outcomes for students will be part of the story though we also need to make the argument on self-interest. The upsides should include greater clarity of expectations and the prospect of a more combined effort to achieve good outcomes not the aggregation of individuals' idiosyncratic experiences. More financially resilient institutions will be better for everyone. It will take brave leadership to see through change.

University education, typically delivered in the form of degrees, is already on the road to being seen throughout institutions as a product. I think that this needs to go much further – and more quickly – in institutions so that they reap the potential benefits of productising their offer. I see benefits for students in more consistently high-quality propositions with better structured systematic engagement of their needs as consumers. For institutions, treating education as a product will better arm them to manage the product cycle, delivery costs, and pricing. They should be able to avoid the accidental subsidy for unsuccessful programmes in favour of planned and considered support for the right portfolio. It is only through great products that we can serve students' needs in a mass system.

What about students?

Universities ask a lot of students when they offer degrees. They are, in most cases, seeking money either through the direct payment of tuition fees or via a loan repayment mechanism. They also place burdens and restrictions on what students can do with the time; the opportunity costs of undertaking a degree are significant, not least because, for many students, they will have only one experience of HE through a bachelor's degree. It may not technically be 'one shot', but that is the reality for most people, in practice. This is a huge responsibility for universities, and one which they must meet by doing everything possible within their powers to ensure that the degree fits well with what the student wants to achieve. The value which the student places on the degree might come from the content, the signal value of the certificate, the educational experience, the peri-educational or co-curricular activities, networks, or other aspects of the offer. With students taking different value from their experience, and potentially with changing views on where they receive value over time, universities should be clear about their distinctive proposition. And they must deliver on the promise.

Universities have traditionally been supply-led in their education delivery. When given the freedom to recruit students into whichever programmes they can recruit for, even in capped systems, institutions have shaped the 'offer' to the market largely by what they have the expertise to deliver through traditional, usually siloed, academic departments. This makes sense if it doesn't matter what a student studies, just that they went to the university to get a degree; and there isn't anything else more valuable at the intersection of disciplines. Even where universities have offered degrees across disciplines, these often fail to satisfy students because the administrative impediments of studying across areas of the university make it a net negative experience, whatever the advantages of the varied content. This siloed supply and lack of imagination has dominated the undergraduate offer more than the postgraduate. In the undergraduate system, typically with a regulated unit of resource for the institutions, there has been less imperative to innovate compared to the postgraduate space with uncapped fees and, therefore, greater potential upside to offering something attractive to the market. Smaller minimum viable cohorts for master's degrees have also made it easier for universities to put on a wider range of programmes.

The supply-led model has its benefits. First, it speaks to a key, distinctively positive dimension of universities: providing education in their areas of expertise. If they have a chemistry department populated by chemists with experience of research and teaching, then it makes sense of offer a suite of chemistry-related degrees. If at the heart of the education experience is some transmission of knowledge, and development of skills to access and apply that knowledge, then there must be some point at which it was known. The supply-led model also benefits institutions, as it means that they can align the delivery of the teaching component of education to the departmental structure delivered, in the main, by academics whose roles require them to do both teaching and research. These core academics are supplemented by permanent teaching-focussed colleagues, and by sessionals or adjuncts, but the point is that the course is built around the expertise of those academics in established positions. There may, too, be benefits to students in having a disciplinary 'home' for their programme and a tangible sense of being part of a community of scholars.

Many university leaders speak of the connection of research and teaching as a fiction, or at least as something with only a loose connection. Most courses in universities cover similar ground to each other, and are not directly connecting the research taking place within that institutional setting to the education delivery. There are many highly successful teaching-focussed universities with little research effort able to deliver high-quality courses which draw on the latest scholarship in the discipline to provide students with a relevant and academically rigorous experience. We need to get over the increasingly old-fashioned idea that research and education have to be connected within the same physical space, or connected by the same individual. Many researchers make poor teachers. We still need research-informed education, and the best people to develop and deliver that education are those who can translate the research. We need to accept that these translators may not be the researchers themselves, and it is within the large universities where we can afford this differentiation of roles through specialisation.

It is possible, however, to imagine a different starting point for the design and delivery of a university education which starts not with 'what the university has to teach', but with 'what the student wants to learn', and 'how can that need be met'. Many institutions will speak to student-centricity, but fail to take the approach to its natural conclusion of interrogating how students benefit from their education, and building experiences – teaching and learning, but much beyond this to the fully rounded experiences – which meet, or ideally exceed, those needs. This does not mean abandoning all principles, or dumbing down. A university without the ability to speak to the unpopular or controversial is a university which fails to deliver its maximum value. Learning needs to be challenging for students to receive the most value. And this is all the more necessary to meet evolving student needs, including for the future of work. Providing flexibility and convenience in education, including through a variety of delivery modes including fully-online programmes, should not be seen as a threat to the university but the key to unlock the potential of the future university. What might have been innovation at the margins of the university should not be the core.

The best products deliver positive outcomes for students

In general, there's not a lot of booing at graduation ceremonies. But in one university, when any reference is made to a survey course introduced by the institution ostensibly for students' benefit, the course gets jeered at graduation. The course was introduced to give students more access to the university's top professors and to show students the breadth of what is possible across the institution's disciplines. It was created in response to students' feedback. Many students hated it. This should not have been a surprise, given that students often see anything which isn't what they had 'bought' – the named title of the course that they have signed up to – as a barrier to their success. The institution may have been right, intellectually, that this breadth of disciplinary knowledge would be the right thing for students. At graduation they were not happy, but perhaps later in life they will see the value of this broadening of their horizons. The change to create this variant of 'the product' didn't seem to have a detrimental effect on the recruitment of students, but it shows a mismatch between what students expected and what they got. It also shows how important it is to truly understand students' feedback to ensure that responses address their complaints, rather than introduce new issues.

***

Many working in and around HE may find the idea of thinking of education as a product uncomfortable. The tradition of the cottage industry with flexibility and nuance, and the mystique of the sage professor, provide a background conception of what a university education looks like. But this is true not across the sector but more typically in traditional, research-intensive institutions. Teaching-focussed universities have embraced more product-led approaches, in part out of the necessity of more constrained funding, but they, too, would benefit from the further extension of this approach. In the future which I imagine, the cottage industry version will still exist, but it will be there only in those over-funded hyper luxury universities which contribute so little to enabling the success for the many through massified HE. Universities need to offer education to the mass of the population with reasonable costs; they, therefore, need ways to scale efficiently.

If we can reach a point where education meets students' needs, and where it can be delivered efficiently, it may be that we can address a core issue in the sector, which is the constant criticism that it does not provide value for money, for any party. We can get the best of all worlds with supportive policymakers, great outcomes for students, and with the distributable revenue to support research where it can be most impactful. I also argue that this approach does not mean that the merciless bean counters have won. My proposal doesn't just focus on the economic returns to the individual either. I am making the case for a fuller understanding of why a student would invest their time and money in studying any particular course. What is valuable to the individual student may be the purely financial return on that investment, and that is a perfectly reasonable position for the student to take. Equally, they may value the experience, access to a profession, the connection with others, the intellectual challenge. The features of the product may be important, such as the convenience to study locally, or online, or to pursue a flexible programme with many options.

The features of the fully productised education offer should include:

- **A centrally planned approach** to deciding what to offer, not left to departmental proposals, to ensure that business cases are sound and that each course contributes to the core across a combination of financial, reputational, and social dimensions.
- **Professional product management** which takes potential courses from hypothesis to fruition quickly, using dedicated resources, not time borrowed from within a department.

- **Intensive qualitative and quantitative market research** to understand diverse students' needs and how they may be met, including across global markets where appropriate, and anticipating needs as well as reflecting existing market demand.
- **A robust business case process** which evaluates the costs of creation and delivery of the course, assesses potential demand and the costs of recruiting students, and only approves courses where they make a material financial contribution or where an investment case is made for benefits beyond financial outcomes.
- **Active engagement with professional, statutory, and regulatory bodies, and with employers and their representatives**, to understand changing needs in professions and how universities can best meet them through education, whether degrees or other formats.
- **Integration of the best scholarship and research** to ensure that the university lives up to the promise to provide students academically rich and relevant experiences.
- **Testing and piloting new concepts**, for example, through short courses or options within existing courses, to establish potential demand in areas where there is no existing provision.
- **Marketing and recruitment which speaks to the distinctive student value proposition** based on what they will receive from the experience and outcomes.
- **Setting entry standards and expectations** which enable students to succeed, and offering pathways into courses for students who would benefit from foundational or bridging provision.
- **Standardised delivery structures**, including credit weightings, assessment volumes, learning resources, and course rhythms to deliver efficient and consistent experiences which are easier to manage for the university.
- **Resilient delivery models** not reliant on individuals' knowledge and experience but where everyone is replaceable in pursuit of continuity for students.
- **Great learning technologies** to ensure that students have scalable high quality learning experiences. The data from engagement should inform how the university optimises product development and delivery.
- **Integration of real-world experiences** which are directly relevant to students' outcomes, balancing that which is provided within the university and how learning can be achieved in other settings.

- **Choice in the student journey** which allows for flexibility about their experience, within frameworks, and for choice without being overwhelmed by options, while ensuring the coherence of the course.
- **Training and development for educators** to scaffold their experiences and ensure that product expectations are clear, with provision of the tools which enable staff to meet or exceed those expectations.
- **Live intelligence which demonstrates the performance of a course** for academic, experiential, and commercial outcomes to enable monitoring and intervention as necessary.
- **Wraparound support for students and staff** to ensure that issues flagged are addressed quickly and effectively throughout, and that insights from how people experience the education are taken into account for future iterations through lessons learned.
- **Annual and periodic reviews** to refresh, renew, or retire courses, avoiding a set-and-forget mentality to implement a true product cycle.
- **Supporting students following completion** through career advisory services and active alumni networks.

***

In the productised model, it is not only those programmes that deliver high financial surpluses which get approved. The university can – and should – also deliver programmes which contribute to the institution's unique context. But the key difference is that these investments can be understood, rather than the accidental subsidy for unsuccessful areas of provision.

The centralised approach requires nuances at disciplinary levels to ensure that the experience of teaching and learning meets the needs of that specific programme. This would be achieved through the project management methodology to develop courses where a qualified third-space professional,[25] such as learning designers, support subject matter experts to bring their content to life. The allocation of resources for product development can be regularised fully to understand the costs and, with that, the business case can be built for any given programme. This standardisation of approach also benefits the university in its ability to institute whole-institution initiatives where it chooses. For example, a university could systematically decolonise

---

25 See Celia Whitchurch's work, including *Reconstructing Identities in higher education: The rise of third space professionals*, London and New York: Routledge, 2013.

its curricula through the project management of new programmes, and then through each product as it came due for renewal, by ensuring that the project management methodology required experts to reflect upon, and respond to, the need for more diverse representation (at a minimum), with advice and guidance for developing anti-racist curricula.

Few, if any, universities can point confidently to the facts on the cost of the design and delivery of their education. Without this information, they cannot know for certain where their margins are made, and they cannot optimise for the greatest positive impact. That impact will, in part, be the surpluses generated for reinvestment in the institution. It should also be those areas where students benefit most – on their own terms – from the university's education. This approach may horrify some in the sector as a heartless denuding of that which is special about a university education. I argue the opposite: this approach is absolutely essential if we are to have any universities at all.

Universities need to change

The productisation of the education offer is predicated on a radical mindset shift for universities. To reach the point I have proposed, where market needs (as expressed in the benefit which should accrue to those who study on the course) guide the development, testing, refinement, delivery, and ongoing management of degrees, the ways of working in the university must change. The most fundamental of these changes is the shift to seeing education at a corporate activity, and not an individual one. We need to accept that research and education are connected, but not necessarily because both activities are conducted by the same person. The university corporately should own the intellectual property of a degree programme, should be responsible for the costs of its creation and delivery, and should reap the ongoing benefits of its success for the greater purpose of the university as a platform. The education delivered is not the space in which academic freedom is paramount; yes, there will be freedom to shape any given teaching interaction according to preferences and expertise, but that would be within narrow bounds focussed on deliver of a consistently high-quality experience. And if you don't like it, there are two options: enjoy the academic freedoms and personal gain which come from academic research, or find a teaching role in one of those increasingly old-fashioned institutions which pitch eclectic amateur teaching as part of their old-world charm.

The university with the fully productised education offer, the one which optimises its portfolio to generate significant surpluses for reinvestment in research, should have a positive story to tell its communities. The staff who teach, i.e., who may be employed just to teach, or occupy that role combined with research, should be well-remunerated, have appropriate time allocations to do the work, and have clear progression opportunities. They should find joy in their work. It will be much clearer in my proposed future who is performing well, and who less well, and it will also be clearer at the institutional level how proportionate pay and conditions can be built into the business case. With clear rules on the scalability of programmes, universities should not have the issue of over-stretching colleagues through over-recruitment of students. Staff who specialise in teaching through this model, and the other colleagues like the expert product managers, should also have significant power to command good conditions, as their work will be more tangibly recognised. It should also be easier to compare the respective offers of different institutions, and to make comparisons between working in university teaching and roles outside the sector. The future university should take pride in the quality of its staff experience, as well of that of students, and structure its modelling to ensure that good work is rewarded, and inadequate work is not.

Universities clearly need analytical tools to manage their product portfolios and at-scale delivery. The self-optimising university will use the quantitative and qualitative insights for continuous improvement. We know, however, that these systems have been deficient in many ways, not least because they pose risks for under-valuing the work of women and people of colour. As institutions work on developing in this area, they need to find ways to use the tools to fight, and not confirm, social inequalities and un/conscious biases. There is also a strong need for rich and deep engagement with staff and students to interrogate the experience and understand the real nuances behind the data. There will remain a vitally important role for students' active engagement in shaping their educational experiences, individually and collectively. The students' union need not become a consumer rights organisation denuded of campaigning activism; the broader experience of the university, and that which makes it special, includes the opportunities for representation and engagement with the institution at different levels. These should be nurtured to reflect the human side of education which will remain essential for success: in my future university, the robots have not come for all the jobs... yet.

What would be different in the future university?

- Students are consistently delighted with the quality of their education and experience because it has been designed and delivered in ways which suit their needs. There is the right balance between standardisation of delivery – supporting efficiency – and personalisation to ensure that each and every individual can succeed.
- Universities clearly own the delivery of education as a corporate responsibility, not an individual academic one. Academic and professional staff know what is expected of them in terms of service expectations and they deliver the quality expected of them and which is consistent with the value proposition for students.
- Academic portfolios are diverse. They provide students with choice and manage the institution's exposure to changing demand in any given area. The university balances margin-generating programmes with emerging areas requiring pump-priming and deliberate investment in degrees relevant to the institutional mission.
- Educators take delight in teaching and learning because automation has eliminated routine tasks, leaving space for intellectual challenge and enriching experiences which are underpinned by human connection. Teaching is highly valued and staff have successful careers enabling students to succeed while working within a clear framework.
- Success is measured by the achievement of the intended aims of the programme and broader university value proposition. Satisfaction is important, but we have better measures which focus on the impact of learning and reward those universities which create long-term positive impacts for the people they educate.

***

Universities need free cash to fulfil their mission. With most universities, even research-intensive ones, the bulk of their income is generated from tuition from degrees. It is, therefore, vitally important that these product lines serve the needs of the institution, and they will only do that when they serve well the needs of consumers. This approach does not have to infantilise students or staff. The focus must be on serving needs, including through mind-expanding and engaging experiences, just not ones created by the supply of what universities want to offer the market because of the historical accident of their academic disciplines. With this approach, and the underpinning capabilities to manage the product cycle, universities will be able to run efficiently and build the capacity for reinvestment in their missions. And this is in addition to the direct benefits which they create for students. That reinvestment might be further areas of financially unprofitable but socially valuable education, or in community activities, or into their research efforts. Getting this part right is vital to unlock the full potential of the university.

Make your research portfolio deliberate

Research is an essential component of the university mission and a distinct capability of the institutional form. However, it is an expensive activity and one which requires a risk-weighted investment strategy to provide returns on the investment of external funds and internal allocations. While research could be considered predominantly in business model terms, this needs to be reconciled with the human dimension of building and sustaining a research culture. Universities need to build more joyful workplaces which nurture creativity and promote working to collective ends.

The future university needs both education and research

Universities are collections of people doing many different things. Be it called a cottage industry, a conglomerate of thousands of sole traders, or some other imperfect description of the complexity, the point is made that the institution is a platform for individuals. In the preceding chapter on education, I made the case that the university needs to reject this notion of individualism when it comes to the determination of the course portfolio and the delivery of those courses. The future university must embrace a product strategy if it is to survive, and if it is to grow sustainably to meet the increasing need for higher level skills. This offers a disruptive approach to the way universities have traditionally managed their education. But what about research? The approach needs to be fundamentally different because the approach to value creation is different. For education, it is about delivering on the ambitions and expectations of the individual. For research, we seek benefits for communities, be that from the pure expansion of the sum of knowledge, or from applied interventions which affect lives directly. With a different approach to value, so comes a different approach to structuring the university to create that value.

***

If universities are to work in the marketised system, they need to provide education and conduct research. If they exist just to do teaching – even in the productised mode – they might well get undone by competition which seeks to find, and compete with, the most profitable parts of their portfolios. But those competitors will not also be the generators of knowledge. For the university to work, it needs to connect the principles of the creation of knowledge with the transmission through structured education products. It is the university which employs both educators and researchers which will be best able to ensure that its products are at the forefront of scholarship, and through that, with the connections to industry and the broader world outside the institution, they will deliver value for students.

Research is also critical to the business model for the creation of the positive benefits for society. It is the point of the mission of the university, and not something which would ever be completely displaced by stand-alone research institutes, private research and development activities, or other forms of contracted research. Those will all have their parts to play within the ecosystem of research but they, in their current forms, will be limited in their options for interdisciplinarity, and by their scale. They are also more limited in their business models; the investment of tuition surplus into research is one of the key efficiencies of the university. The university creates value in the education offer, captures a portion of that value as surplus, and reinvests that into the research effort. This should not be considered a bad thing, so long as universities genuinely create that value for students in the education offer as proposed. The student receives value from the degree greater than the cost of delivering that service. The university, fulfilling its public purpose, applies that surplus for good, rather than extracting it as profit.

I made the case for a radical approach to the creation of education products, one which takes what some universities have started but which few have seen through to fruition. This will alarm many in the sector who value the flexibility in current approaches. In contrast, research needs to be liberated rather than constrained. For teaching, the focus on effective andragogy is paramount, and while there will be nuances around the transmission of knowledge and the development of skill in different subject areas, there will be more commonality than divergence. By contrast, the disciplines of research have greater differences which need to be respected. More fundamentally though, successful research relies on cultures, resources, and environments which provide the conditions for the exploration and communication of ideas, and the generation of new knowledge.

It is not just the happy accident of surplus reallocation which makes universities the places where the old knowledges are held and preserved, and these new knowledges are created. Universities provide the infrastructure of policies, financial management, guidelines for performance, and good practice which can enable researchers to flourish, within some necessary constraints. This is the theory, at least. For the university to succeed, it must see the task as creating the best conditions for success. Where the corporate task in education is consistency and rigour, the task in research is to provide the minimum constraint which allows people to find joy and to flourish as researchers. At the micro level, this means recruiting and nurturing the best talent, and at a meso-level, universities need to determine which broad areas of research should form part of the portfolio appropriate to the time and place in which they operate. An honest recognition of the roles and responsibilities of the university, and how these differ across the missions, is vital, if institutions are to find consistent success.

Structures and incentives need to better align for successful research

It is often said in universities than an academic's loyalty is first to themselves, then to the discipline, and somewhere down a long list of affiliations comes the institution from which they draw a salary. In the case of the education offer of a university, there is a strong business case for challenging that relationship and demonstrating the value of the common and corporate ends rather than the individual. But when it comes to research, we may need to embrace the independence and agency of the researcher – to work with the grain of the norms and expectations of academic freedom and culture – to get the most value for all beneficiaries. In my model future university, the core incentives for research will need to reward individual success, with the market for academic research serving to promote competition between institutions to offer the best environments to which researchers choose to affiliate for some time.

Academic research is a people business, and for many is it a vocation or lifestyle which transcends any conception of a nine-to-five working pattern.

This is core to why academic and professional staff have different roles and expectations: for many academics, it is the university alone which provides the conditions in which they can fully realise their vocation. Professional staff should much more easily be able to translate their skills into parallel roles in other organisations. They can both find joy, but the motivations and conditions are different. In many universities, long-retired members of academic departments continue to participate in the intellectual life of the institution because the urge to continue exploring the frontiers of knowledge is simply what they are wired to do. For the research part of a university to work, we need to embrace the vocational element and not eliminate all pleasure from the activity through unhelpful measurement exercises manifesting in audit cultures, or burdensome bureaucracies which make simple tasks difficult. Pay and conditions must also match the vocational dimension of the researcher's endogenous needs and wants. Universities should embrace the fact that their academic staff have motivations which go beyond pay, and that institutions can offer them the environments in which they do their best work.

In this context it is important that intellectual property remains with the researcher. Universities should be able to take stakes in innovative developments where they are commercialised but the core incentives are for individuals, and groups of collaborating individuals, to develop and exploit the ideas which have their names on them. Success will come from liberation within clear structures and incentives.

Research should be in proportion to institutional mission

One vice-chancellor at a very old university delighted in telling the story that the inability of the university to make decisions meant that it had retained a plant sciences research unit which had been threatened with closure in the twentieth century. Come the twenty-first century, a renewed interest in plant sciences made it one of the exciting areas for new developments. Few universities can afford such accidental bounties which come from the luxury of hanging around long enough that an area of research will be considered interesting or valuable again. But this is a case for the inefficiency of universities – particularly in the case of their research infrastructure and expertise – which allows for a range of possible futures.

At the individual level, research should be liberated to allow researchers to do their things as well as possible. But the university has a role to set the parameters in which it seeks to conduct research – the disciplines in which it will invest –

and the proportion of the activity that research will make up. There will need to be some alignment to the education effort to retain credibility in the education offer, though it does not need to be the case that the volume of funded research, as measured in people effort or in cash terms, is evenly in proportion to the volume of students or revenue from tuition. Ultimately, the volume of research will be largely determined by the combined potential investment from block-grant funding and the surpluses generated from the teaching effort. While competitive grant funding is also an important component, rather than see this as additional, universities understand this as a co-investment or match funding model which makes the institution's own investment go further, but it is the output of the investment strategy, rather than the input resource for investment.

Investment approaches will help universities think about their portfolios

The university's research portfolio is less like a single business than it is an investment fund. It is the aggregation of many diverse activities which happen to be conglomerated for the purposes of reporting but which are largely independent. Rather than think of the university simply as a passive investment vehicle spreading its funds evenly across a set of options like an index tracker, the university could be more like a managed fund which chooses where, and how much, to invest across its myriad potential activities. Some might argue that this is what universities currently do, but in my experience the current approach is much more accidental than designed. Financial models within universities are often led too directly by the education revenue – which I propose removing to an institution level – and there is the serendipitous co-investment in researchers who win grants with the university expected to foot whatever bill remains because different funders contribute idiosyncratically to overheads. I'm proposing a considered and deliberate investment strategy to overcome the risk that the current haphazard approach has; the accidental investment approach will not create the most value for society.

Research is, by its nature, a risky investment. We cannot predict with absolute certainty how successful any given research activity will be. Nor are we agreed on what success looks like. For any given input – researcher time, equipment, networks – we do not know what the result will be. This is an element of the excitement in research and precisely why universities exist. They need to be the places in which hypotheses are developed and tested. Some well-established research areas may be more predictable than others, but all are working within significant uncertainty. There is also the question of what is considered success: the investment into research should generate value, which may be in the intellectual contribution to a discipline, or the development of a concept or technology which can be applied outside the university, or a public policy or health intervention. The value of research is in its impact.

The impact may not be immediate. The investment approach in a university needs to consider the reality that research will mature at different rates. In practice, the deliberate investment approach means that a university would set out its broad parameters for investment: it should take a stance on the proportion it seeks to invest in high-risk activities – low probability of success, but high potential reward – and those areas which are more likely to generate a more predictable return. This should be assessed both by the field in which the research is proposed as well as the researchers making the proposition; a researcher with a strong track record is likely, though not guaranteed, to have success again. An early-career researcher may be rated as higher risk, but a risk worth taking because of the potential reward.

The mechanism for investment in a university's research portfolio begins with an application process. Researchers submit proposals detailing their intended projects, including research goals, methodologies, anticipated outcomes, and projected costs. The evaluation of these applications should not solely rest on potential immediate benefits or superficial metrics; instead, a more nuanced, risk-weighted model should be employed. This model would take into account various factors, including the potential for ground-breaking results, the alignment with the institution's strategic research focus, and the project's risk profile, which could consider the project's complexity, the researcher's track record, and other relevant factors.

The allocation of investments is a strategic decision that should be made with a long-term perspective. Universities need to consider their commitments over different timeframes – say, three, five, 10, or even 20 years – weighing the risk and potential of each investment. This might involve committing to a number of research positions over several years or capital investments to enhance research capabilities. And it's essential to reserve some funds for co-investment in externally funded research. Although such schemes can suffer from low success rates, they can also offer opportunities for leverage and partnerships that can augment the university's research capabilities and reach. Universities might also club together to make combined investments following the example of London's Francis Crick Institute for biomedicine which is a collaboration between three universities, two charities, and a research funding body.

Implementing a risk-weighted investment model also allows for more meaningful engagement between institutional leaders and researchers. By discussing the potential risks and rewards of different research projects, leaders can develop a deeper understanding of each discipline's nuances, and researchers can better understand the institutional strategy and constraints. This dialogue should lead to a shared understanding of the investment decisions and foster a sense of ownership and alignment across the university. With a risk-weighted investment model, researchers would be incentivised to deliver high-quality outputs, because future investments would depend on their results, or at least the story which they can tell from past successes and failures and how those experiences inform their future plans. This encourages accountability, as well as promoting healthy internal competition for resources. However, the incentives need to be balanced to ensure this system doesn't create undue pressure or encourage short-term thinking that could compromise the quality of research. We need to be measured in the investments, and not just fund those with the biggest claims.

There is a danger that some research areas could become underfunded in this model. Yet, this could also provide market opportunities for other institutions, thereby promoting diversity and dynamism in the overall research landscape. Furthermore, institutions may want to maintain a minimum level of activity in each discipline to deliver a well-rounded education and maintain credibility across broad areas of study.

Creating a more sustainable and strategic research funding model requires a shift in mindset and practice. It involves recognising and respecting the diversity of academic disciplines, acknowledging the inherently uncertain nature of research, and committing to long-term investments. The approach should be consistent with developing cultures of joy within the academic profession. Being accountable for the investment in your research area should be consistent with a joyful experience; there will always be some hurdles to overcome, but if they provide the freedom to do one's best work, then the effort to obtain the investment will be worth it. It is making the case for the research and receiving the freedom to pursue those goals which will create the conditions in which researchers can flourish. Universities need vibrant, productive, and sustainable research environments, which will, in turn, attract, nurture, and retain the best talent. And with that talent, universities will deliver on their mission, creating benefit for society.

What would be different in the future university?

- There is a widespread recognition that value creation through research is inherently risky with the potential for benefits only to be recognised long after work is conducted. This risk mindset drives the investment approach, resulting in a balanced portfolio of research investments which aim to deliver benefits over the short, medium, and long terms.
- Researchers are empowered to make the case for their research within a university by articulating its importance in a field or discipline, for commercial applications where appropriate, and for the benefit of society. While research has many diverse activities and target benefits, universities have mechanisms which evaluate the relative merits of investment cases and make transparent decisions about their investment strategies.
- Universities give their funded researchers the freedom and resources to do their best work, collaborating within the institution and beyond in pursuit of the greatest advancement of knowledge or practice. Researchers find joy in their activities which are demonstrably part of the university's mission of creating value for communities.
- Researchers bid for external funds where the university has determined that pursuit fits with the investment strategy, knowing in full the co-investment required for successful bids. Researcher performance is not measured by bids submitted, or even funding won, but by the quality and impact of their work and how their efforts create value.

***

Research is fundamental to the good created by universities, and we should focus on securing the conditions for optimal success. That means finding ways to liberate researchers to do what is best in their specific contexts, without too strong a focus on the inputs. Institutions will invest their own, and others', money – translated into time and facilities – to seek returns through the impact of research on the discipline and in wider society. With a risk-weighted investment approach which recognises the time it will take to see return – providing researchers with enough runway during which to demonstrate results – it allows for deliberate decision making. All of this needs to sit within the principle of creating joyful places in which research can flourish.

Benefit your communities

The third component of the university mission is the creation of social impact. This has often been an afterthought in institutions focussed too squarely on education and research. Universities as ivory towers have been exclusive places with high walls, often literally but also figuratively in terms of access to their intellectual assets. For universities to be relevant in the future, and not just organisations which compete in the open market with for-profit providers, they need to be cultural beacons. Communities should be proud of what universities do, how they provide social infrastructure, preserve and share knowledge, and contribute to a greater good. They should be spaces of debate and the sharing of ideas, and also be places which are safe and respectful. While presented as concepts in conflict, these are consistent ideals.

The impactful university

Universities need to be more deliberate in their pursuit of social impacts, not just assuming that these are nice-to-have spill-over benefits. There has long been a 'third leg' or 'third stream' within university strategies which has encompassed a broader engagement with community. This might manifest as a 'service' culture and mandate, a 'civic' commitment or some other expression of coordination of activities. In *The Purpose-Driven University*, Debbie Haski-Leventhal connects the benefits of a purposeful strategic approach to students' increasing desire for purposeful careers, the broader Environmental, Social and Governance (ESG) agenda and institutional ethics. Her definition is: "A purpose-driven university utilises its resources, knowledge, talent, and people to continuously and intentionally contribute to the communities and the environment in which it operates: through research, education, programmes, and service."[26] She further makes the case for measuring and communicating social impact to tell powerful stories about the value of universities. I have written of social impact as the third part of the university mission to focus attention on that active word 'impact'. I use this to imply a considered and purposeful approach which draws attention to the benefits created.

The case for the deliberate development of an impactful university, one which creates much more value than the sum of its parts, has multiple features:

- **Seek positive outcomes for communities:** universities can use their resources and expertise to address local and global challenges. By engaging with their communities, universities can have a significant impact on issues such as poverty, inequality, and environmental sustainability. Universities should be leaders across the full breadth of potential impacts, such as those expressed in the UN Sustainable Development Goals (SDGs).
- **Democratise knowledge to enrich lives:** universities can contribute to making knowledge more accessible and understandable to the public, thereby fostering an informed society. This also supports the goal of attracting students to study in universities, and in demonstrating the attractiveness of academic careers to support future generations of talented educators and researchers.
- **Make education and research relevant:** universities which are connected to communities can more easily ensure that their education and research have purpose and reflect trends and issues in society. This does not always mean following society; it may also mean leading the development of ideas which support social progress.
- **Pursue higher quality educational experiences:** universities need students to have meaningful and impactful learning experiences, and not just those which happen within the confines of the institution's digital or physical spaces. Community-connected curricula will better prepare graduates for their future careers.
- **Produce quality applied research and innovation:** universities should address the issues and challenges in society, and they can only do that if they have in place mechanisms for engaging communities. This includes

---

26 Debbie Haski-Leventhal (2020). *The Purpose-Driven University: Transforming Lives and Creating Impact Through Higher Education*. Emerald Publishing, p14.

the capacity for knowledge transfer and ensuring systematically that the insights created in the university can be applied beyond broadly.
- **Share responsibility for progress:** universities do not exist in isolation but are institutions intimately connected with, and the product of, communities. There is a moral duty to fulfil the full potential of the public-purpose university.

By engaging effectively with their communities, universities maximise their impact, remain responsive to societal needs, and enhance their education and research. The impactful university creates purpose for students and staff and supports joyful work. A focus on social impact creates the synergistic relationship which benefits communities, the university, and broader society.

The truthful university

When England's Office for Students appointed Arif Ahmed, Professor of Philosophy at the University of Cambridge, as Director for Freedom of Speech and Academic Freedom in June 2023, he wrote for *The Times* that:

> *A university is not a club. It is not a political lobby. It is not a seminary. It is not a 'brand'. It exists to seek and speak truth, whatever it costs and whoever it upsets. Therefore, without freedom to explore controversial or 'offensive' ideas, a university is nothing.*

If you've read this far, you'll know that I disagree. A university is a club, a place which one can join and where membership carries rights and responsibilities. Universities are also able to make political points, or at least they should as they relate to good policymaking in HE. As for a seminary, I don't care either way. And a brand? Yes, definitely. Universities have corporate identities which are enormously important and they need ways in which to communicate what they offer to the outside world. You might not like the word 'brand', but it fits the bill. Where Ahmed and I might find common ground is that universities exist to seek and speak truth, and they need to explore the controversial, and that which might be considered offensive, though there has to be limits and guardrails. And I don't think that it should cause controversy to say that harmful and upsetting speech, where avoidable, should be avoided.

It is hard to find a news article about universities which doesn't decry the end of free speech and how 'snowflake' students have taken over. It doesn't actually matter whether there truly is a 'chilling effect' caused by 'no platforming' or 'cancel culture': these are terms in the common discourse on the contemporary university, and we have to consider what they mean and how to find a way through the debate.

***

'Academic freedom' and 'freedom of expression' are both fundamental principles in a university setting, but they apply to different contexts and carry different implications.

> **Academic freedom** typically refers to the rights of academics and, to some extent, students in a university context. It includes the freedom to conduct research, publish, and discuss topics in teaching without facing restraint or reprisal from the institution of their employment or wider society. The purpose of academic freedom is to ensure that academics can pursue truth and contribute to the body of human knowledge without undue influence or pressure from outside entities. This includes researching controversial topics or holding controversial perspectives based on the researcher's understanding of their field of study. Academic freedom is subject to certain limitations. For example, academics must still adhere to the standards and ethics of their respective fields, as well as the regulations of their institution. They are also expected to teach material that is relevant to their course topics, and their research is subject to peer review and criticism.
>
> **Freedom of expression** is a more general principle which applies not just to academics but to everyone. It is the right to hold and express opinions without censorship or fear of retaliation. In a university context, it refers to the ability of students, academics, staff, and other members of the university community to freely express their ideas and beliefs, whether in classroom discussions, speeches, writings, art, or other forms of communication. Freedom of expression is also subject to limitations. For example, universities can set reasonable time, place, and manner restrictions on speech. They can also limit or prohibit speech which constitutes a true threat, harassment, or other behaviour that infringes on the rights of others or disrupts the educational environment.

In practice, universities find balancing the support for both academic freedom and freedom of expression mostly very easy. This is what universities are for, and how they go about their business enabling the free exchange of ideas. But these concepts have been weaponised, and there are people within universities and outside who choose to use one or both of these concepts to mislead and to advance their agendas under a veil of legitimacy provided by a university. If proof were needed that universities have an intangible value, it is that actors seek to weaponise them.

The challenges come in a variety of forms. In some cases, speakers with hateful messages seek to speak at universities, either to use a public platform to spread bile, or to enjoy the social media pile-on if they are challenged or cancelled. This is now a regular win–win strategy for those who wish to take advantage of universities which feel unable to prevent speakers who bring nothing useful or positive. There is also a challenge for universities from those in academic positions whose practice is advocacy for one side of a political debate or another. It is too easy to dress up ideology in academic garb and, if challenged by the discipline, to claim that this is the system ganging up on someone trying to speak truth.

Universities need to have clear definitions and policies on both academic freedom and freedom of expression. But this goes nowhere near far enough to help everyone – inside the university, and outside, in the broader community – to really understand what is true, and what is important. Truth is an elusive concept, and what is truthful today may not be truthful tomorrow if new evidence unfolds and we have to reassess. If they are to have any positive social impact at all, universities need to see part of their role as helping us seek and find truth, and to understand what is not truthful. In practice, this means investing in debate such that hateful views are challenged robustly and in real time, not rising to specious arguments but taking the heat out of the controversial. It means helping to educate everyone on what it means to understand evidence and to weigh it. It also means bringing disciplines together to understand complex issues from a range of perspectives.[27]

It is not acceptable for universities to shy away from difficult debates, however hard they may find them and how challenging to navigate. Academics

---

27 One of the front lines of the culture wars and their intersection with universities is trans rights. This is a classically difficult issue for universities, because there are multiple 'sides' and diverse arguments cutting across gender studies, sociology, biology, law, and so on. And there is a need to protect members of the community – both trans and not trans – enabling people to be happy, healthy, and safe. Where universities fail is when they allow the 'debate' to be too simplistic, to allow them to be positioned on a 'side', when the reality is more complex, not least in this case how neo-fascists weaponise trans rights in a basket of otherwise unrelated issues.

and professional staff, beyond those specialising in media, need to have the tools and approaches to know how to navigate the controversial before they are overwhelmed by the deluge. We should provide space for debate and exploration of ideas. Universities need to be places in society where debate takes place, just not uncritically. Without push-back, universities will continue to fall victim to those agents who use the university as a platform for hate. We need to be better than that.

The engaged university

The concept of community engagement is not new, but neither has it traditionally been a primary focus in the HE sector. Engagement is typically seen as an ancillary function of the university, a helpful but not essential part of the institution's role in society. We need to assert its position at the heart of university strategy. The potential benefits of a strategic, university-wide focus on community engagement are enormous and transformational, both for the institutions and the communities which they serve. Through active engagement, universities have the opportunity to connect more deeply with their communities, enhancing their reputations, promoting social inclusivity, and enriching the student experience. Students and staff will be more socially aware, fostering an institutional culture that values social responsibility. It also ensures that the fruits of education and research are shared more equitably, contributing to social justice and societal development.

Community engagement also carries risks. There is a delicate balance to strike between active engagement and the maintenance of a university's role as a space for intellectual independence, academic freedom, and unbiased inquiry. The question arises whether universities, known for promoting discourse and academic freedom, should find themselves seemingly supporting one side or another in community or political issues. In the face of this complexity, it's crucial for universities to develop an engagement model that respects their commitment to impartiality while meaningfully contributing to their communities. There are contrasting models to consider in this context.

The UK's Civic University Network provides a more top-down institutional model of engagement, while Jonathan Grant's *The New Power University* suggests more of a bottom-up approach, driven by distributed models and the initiatives of individuals and smaller groups within and connected to the institution. The Network's model sees the university as a 'steward' of place, directing its resources strategically towards the needs of its local community. On the other hand, Grant encourages grassroots innovation and engagement, suggesting that true societal impact is achieved when individuals at all levels of the university engage with their communities. Both the top-down and bottom-up models have their strengths. The institutional approach ensures that community engagement is woven into the fabric of the university's strategic plan. It ensures a unified, well-coordinated effort that can deliver large-scale impact. The bottom-up approach, however, allows for a wider range of engagement activities, harnessing the diverse interests and skills of the university community.

The contrasting but potentially complementary models highlight that community engagement can be pursued in different ways, but what matters is that it should be embedded into the ethos of a university. It is not an add-on to the traditional focus areas of education and research but, rather, a critical component of a modern university's mission. Public-purpose universities, as part of their social contract, must place community engagement and commitment to place at the heart of their operations. The specific approach may vary based on the institution's context, resources, and community needs. Still, the principle remains: universities, as public-purpose organisations, must seek to benefit communities, explicitly and strategically.

AI is a massive opportunity for universities

Attention to the debate on AI, particularly the advent of freely available generative AI tools like ChatGPT, has focussed too much on the implications of learning and teaching. There is fear that new tools will enable cheating, and that academic standards will be undone by undetectable academic malpractice. It has also been suggested, as part of a narrative of universities' decline, that generative AI will render universities unnecessary, as information flows freely and therefore knowledge can be outsourced. More practically, there is enthusiasm for AI applications within universities to take advantage of their data to make processes more efficient or to enable scaled personalisation for students. These are all valid questions and concerns about the changes that AI has brought into HE, and how things might change in the future. All these questions must also be answered, but too much effort on this subset of the possible misses the enormous opportunity that AI gives universities to assert their relevance to contemporary society.

One of the biggest risks in the development and adoption of AI tools is the inequities they create. Individuals, businesses, and governments will be able to take advantage of increased efficiency where they implement technologies to increase productivity. Universities, too, need to do this, but they also need to help people and organisations to capture the benefits of AI. Wealthier people, and larger and more sophisticated organisations will reap the benefits while others are left behind. If the technology giants, including Microsoft and Google, put effort into commercial gain, their tools will be used best by the highest bidders. Universities must be central to the reaction against the potential for even further concentration of wealth.

In practice, embracing the opportunities to demonstrate social impact in the AI domain would look like this:

- Community outreach to inform the broader population of the potentials – good and bad – of AI developments to ensure that those outside the university are well informed.
- Practical clinics and projects for small- and medium-sized enterprises to help them to identify and implement productivity gains from AI.
- Public leadership in the ethics, governance, and regulation of AI to apply multi-disciplinary research to an emerging question.
- Leadership for schools and the vocational sector to enable other educational institutions, both to benefit from AI tools and help them teach their students about the possibilities.
- Accessible open courses for anyone seeking to upskill, using AI in their practice.

Rather than see AI developments as a threat, universities have the chance to embrace the change and show leadership for society. This is precisely an area where free-market approaches risk inequitable outcomes. True social impact from universities is to spot this likelihood and do everything necessary to ensure equitable outcomes. No-one needs to wait for governments or others to give universities permission: this is what universities are for, and they need to act now.

What would be different in the future university?

- Universities place social impact alongside education and research as core to the mission of the institution. This prominence is reflected in strategies, leadership, and resource allocation.
- Universities are clear about the rights and responsibilities of staff, students, and the broader community as they relate to academic freedom and

freedom of expression. They are places of truth and light, even when the content and conduct of the debate is hard.
- Institutions recognise the importance of both bottom-up and top-down approaches to social impact. They use their institutional capabilities corporately and as a platform to empower communities, within and outwith the university, to make positive impacts in the world.
- Universities identify opportunities, like developments in AI, as ways in which they can create greater social impact, and where their unique capabilities are essential for community success. They do not wait to be told where opportunities lie but seize them as they arise.

***

The future university must be impactful, truthful and engaged. Universities must cement their role as crucial civic and social anchors, and proactive agents for positive change in their communities, aligning their activities with the evolving needs and expectations of society in the face of rapid technological advancements. A reimagined HE system will acknowledge and embrace the critical role of social impact as central to the university mission. The benefits – to universities, to students, to communities – are extensive and compelling. The risks are manageable with thoughtful, inclusive strategies. Universities, in their pursuit of knowledge and innovation, must do so not in isolation but hand-in-hand with the communities in which they exist and serve. By doing so, they not only enrich their communities but also ensure their own continued relevance.

Conclusion

The aim of this book has been to find ways to strengthen the value – and benefits – of public-purpose universities within regulated quasi-market systems. The threats to the unit of resource for education, the interference in research agendas, and the risks from disruptive forces external to the sector are real. But universities are worth fighting for. While this proposed future for universities has many continuities with the present, it also has consequences for stakeholders. In this conclusion, I explore the implications for different groups and outline how I see them each playing a role in the success of the HE sector.

The idea of the university must reconcile with the prevailing conditions

In one English university facing enormous change, its core business having been decimated by changes in the funding landscape, the staff union said – in good faith, I am told – that all would be fine, because the university could just sit out the present situation and wait for a Labour government. The status quo of the quasi-market is an entrenched one, and there is little certainty that a Labour government would change its parameters radically. That English university may be able to look to Australia to see if the Labor government of the 2022 election changes the terms of its HE sector's settlement. The betting is that radical changes are much less likely than amendments here and there. If the quasi-market is here to stay, we have to live with it, and do our best to work within it.

The HE systems of 2050 simply cannot have the levels of participation that were seen in the 1950s. For economic, social, cultural, and personal success, the triumphs of widening participation must continue. HE cannot return to being the preserve of a tiny elite; we will all be the poorer, if that is the case. However, we cannot afford for everyone to enjoy a luxury education, because the national finances won't allow. Given the competing forces of the need for expansion and the imperative to control costs, something must be done. And we need to have a sector which is fit to solve the problems we see all around us: in the climate emergency, technology and ethics, trust in expertise, ageing populations, ethno-nationalism, and so on. For us to reap the benefits of HE, we need to have a functioning system with healthy institutions.

Universities can best serve their missions with a realignment of incentives

There are plenty of consultants' reports which sit, gathering dust, on shelves or languish in electronic folders, never to see the light of day because there is a poor fit between the analysis and the capacity or capability for action. I offer this contribution to the discourse on the future of HE not for the purposes of a discussion point, or to sit amidst a pile of other reading material labelled 'interesting but fundamentally useless'. My challenge to the reader working in the HE sector is to recognise the magnitude of the challenges facing HE, to see the urgency with which solutions are needed, and to act in their own sphere of influence to effect change; if not the ideas in this book, then something else which offers a similarly ambitious plan for change across the core functions of universities. Imagination and dialogue are necessary, but too much talk without action is indulgent.

This book presents a manifesto for change in the HE sector, the better to achieve its purpose and ambitions. Universities should, in their physical and digital spaces, be palaces of learning, of idea generation and exploration, and of serving broader social needs. To meet the challenge of the complex mission, and to make the world a better place, universities need to take steps to ensure their continued viability, and that they maximise the potential benefit to students, the beneficiaries of research, and to broader society. To do this, they need to break the unhelpful tethering of education and research resources. What will benefit students most, and their capacity to pay for that education, is not necessarily in proportion to the benefit that can be generated through research investment. Decoupling these approaches to make education explicitly an institutional endeavour, with research localised and differentiated by discipline, is the foundation of the change which could see resource optimised to create the greatest benefits.

I propose these core steps to set universities on course to deliver the benefits to individuals and broader society, all achievable within the current regulatory and financial constraints:

- **Pursue joy,** recognising that universities need to be humane, respectful, and creative places if they are to survive. HE should be a place where talented people seek to do their best work, and where they find the conditions in which to flourish.
- **Run universities balancing efficiency with inefficiency** to make the most of the regulatory conditions and the capabilities inherent in a learning organisation. Right-size the institution to operate efficiently, including, where appropriate, working with governments and regulators to manage the competitive environment for collective success. Invest creatively to diversify income streams and limit others' rent-seeking. Use experimental tools to optimise for impact across the full breadth of what the institution does and how it works. Use surpluses for targeted investment to fund those things which the market won't.
- **Push productisation of education to the extreme** to deliver high-quality content efficiently and with maximum potential benefit to students. Test and experiment with different approaches, engage students, alumni, and employers throughout, and leverage technologies to deliver consistency. Price competitively, where regulations allow, based on return on investment for students, and deliver surpluses for reinvestment. Set and manage quality thresholds, and develop expert third-space professionals to manage design and delivery.
- **Provide freedom for researchers**, focussing on realistic expectations of outcomes which follow the nuances of disciplinary, and interdisciplinary, needs. Use incentive-setting to focus efforts on quality and impact, and for collaborative as well as individual success. Deploy your investment strategy to differentiate the mission of the university: invest according to your strategy, balancing risk, disciplinary mix, and target benefits. Develop the tools to articulate value for a research area through its disciplinary impact or application. Attract, develop, and retain talent by nurturing positive and respectful cultures, and by enabling joy.

- **Do good along the way** through promoting equity and fairness for students and staff. Deliver tangible benefits to communities and make the most of distinctive convening powers. Challenge orthodoxies and provide places where ideas can be debated in respectful and productive ways. The university exists for people, not concepts, and should operate with humanity and compassion.

The future university can build on the proud legacy of the sector. But it must also recognise the need for change. For that, leaders – academic and professional – and those in governance roles, need the time, space, and foresight to see that change is essential. The current settlement for the sector means that there is significant space within the autonomy provided to institutions for them to define their own destinies. They should also shape the conditions in which they operate by demonstrating the case for any improvement to their financial or regulatory settlements. In some cases, an institution's founding mission may be better served in a new institutional form. All options must be on the table.

The people matter as much as the systems and institutions

Sometimes people ask why it is that I love the HE sector, to which I reply that I don't, or more specifically that I didn't look around the range of places in which to work and choose HE. Like many in the sector, I work in and around HE by accident. But what is clear to me – and what keeps me in the sector – is that I have found a connected, open-minded, creative tribe in which I can rub along. While I have written above about incentives, structures, markets, and financially minded ways of running universities, it is clear to me that effecting change in the sector is about people and the cultures in which those people work. I have touched on some of the people elements, and, below, I expand on those points to describe the impacts of my future university model on some key groups. Inevitably, there are some sweeping generalisations here, and also omissions. The task for the imaginative exploration of the future of the sector is to interrogate what may be the impacts on each group with a view to reinforcing that which is positive about HE and what keeps us working in it.

Students
For students to succeed in the future university, they need to seek – and receive – better information from institutions about the products they are offered. That

information should enable prospective students to decide which route to take, with a full understanding of the direct and opportunity costs. Universities need to communicate how the different dimensions of potential value are reflected in the services they provide; this potential disaggregation of the assumed 'this degree will be good for you' into the respective benefits of its component parts enables better decision making. Not all decisions will be perfect, but we can make better judgements about the possible futures with better information.

Students should also engage actively to shape the services that they receive. This may be through the regular feedback mechanisms, where opinions are sought actively; data will also be revealed through behaviour patterns on engagement with the services and resources provided. There will also be opportunities for representative positions at degree level and institutionally, as there are now. Universities should more explicitly see these engagement opportunities as part of the proposition to students – areas in which they might receive value – and support them accordingly. Not only is it right and proper that the student voice is heard, and responded to, but it is important for the business model of the future university. Where these incentives align, and where colleagues understand the imperatives for engagement, the conduct of those interactions should be more positive and productive.

Academic staff
It's not hard to find on social media the reasons why people are #leavingacademia. Excessive workloads, precarious employment, comparatively low pay, and managerialism are all cited as reasons to go. While these expressions of dissatisfaction may represent only a subset of academics' views on the sector, universities need to take heed of the problems that face their academics. In the preceding chapters on education and research, I presented stark implications for changes in the academic conditions at universities. There needs to be a shift for academics working towards explicitly corporate goals in the case of education design and delivery: the provision of degrees is the domain or the institution, not the individual. This may seem to be a concession to the marketised system: it is. However, the corollary is the freedom and flexibility that can be provided when it comes to research careers. The investment portfolio approach proposed above recognises the myriad ways in which academic research does good, for the pure joy in developing new knowledge for the benefit of a discipline to applied research for social, cultural, or economic impact. For the future university to

achieve the richness of its mission, it needs to be both a place of education and a place of research.

The academic career should be a vocation which enables the full expression of individuals' passions for knowledge creation, exploration, and dissemination. Academic staff should have the pay and conditions which provide them with financial security while working with the retirement benefits that enable them to live in comfort. They should also have the leave to recharge their minds and bodies, and workloads which support good health and social and family life beyond work. The future university must not be a place of drudgery.

This future needs to be paid for, and in the massified system, that means the efficient delivery of education at scale. For this, there needs to be new expectations of teaching delivery which reflect the product expectations. Equally, there will be performance expectations in research, though these need to reflect the risks and rewards in the research domain. There should be opportunities for balanced careers across education and research, as well as pathways which are heavily weighted, or exclusive, to one or the other. And academic career development should support colleagues to develop and articulate skills valuable across a range of workplaces, not trapping them in one pathway or sector. Management systems which focus on fairness – with explicit mechanisms for addressing bias – should mean that progression can be based on performance and success.

Universities have not always been respectful workplaces. Workplace relations between academics, and between academic and professional staff, have enabled, rather than challenged, bullying behaviours. This cannot continue. The future university must be a respectful and positive workplace in which all colleagues' contributions are valued and where discrimination on individual characteristics is abhorred. While the structures of the university need to support joy, so, too, do the behaviours of the people within the system.

Professional staff

The complaints about the divide between professional staff and faculty are real. I was once a professional staff member in a couple of universities and witnessed first-hand bullying, contempt, passive resistance, and unchallenged abuse. Much of that reflected entrenched views about the roles of faculty and professional staff. It wasn't all bad, but the complaint about negative aspects of the culture of current universities is real. In the future university which I have proposed, there are new and exciting opportunities for non-academic staff. In particular, the development and status of the third-space roles in the product management and development of curricula should provide significant opportunities for teaching-expert colleagues to deploy brilliant education products which exceed students' needs. These roles are already established, and have become more prominent and significant in the course of universities' responses to the pandemic, but they will have an even more important role in the future.

I have retained a separation between academic and professional careers, not to advance the unhelpful cultural division between these roles; as I note above, there needs to greater respect and positivity across the whole university workforce. I have this separation because, in the main, professional staff have greater opportunities to switch sectors than their academic colleagues. This should also be seen as a more distinctively positive dimension of professional roles and careers with greater encouragement for drawing on the experiences of working in settings other than universities. There are capabilities which are more prevalent in other industries – particularly good commercial skills – from which universities can benefit. Universities which best integrate the experience of those from outside the sector will flourish.

University leaders

It falls to vice-chancellors and their terms to explore the strategies for their universities, to consult on them, and to present the outputs to their communities. These strategies, which all speak to fulfilling the core missions of education and research, are important to set the stage for the following five or 10 years, and they help communicate to colleagues the priorities that particular institution will have beneath the core headlines which are common across the sector. Any leaders who choose to adopt the proposed model for the future university will face challenges in transition, from finding the financial resource to recruiting the talent needed to apply the new model, and shifting the incentives and culture within the university to better enable its long-term success.[28]

The premise of this book is that the marketised system of HE is here to stay, and that, therefore, the task of those working within the conditions set by the architects of the system is to make the best of those conditions. For leaders in universities,

---

28   University leadership has, like the running of universities, been largely an amateur sport. The future university requires a more professional approach; this is not inconsistent with academic leadership, but requires a mindset shift about the importance of running an institution so that it delivers on its mission. One place to start in thinking about university leadership is Tom Kennie and Robin Middlehurst's 2021 *Leadership transitions in universities: Arriving, surviving and thriving at the top*.

this does not mean accepting wholesale and uncritically the minister's or regulator's diktats: leaders should use their influencing capabilities to shape conditions for the better. That will, at times, mean private engagement with policymakers, and also mean engaging with the media, business leaders or civil society groups to make a point through more public means. The subtlety of building coalitions, within and beyond the sector, will be a marker of success for the future university leader. This may be a contrast to conceptions of success which have privileged the vice-chancellor who shouts loudest as the voice of the sector.

My future university also requires some nuanced approaches to leadership, and I propose a greater emphasis on the long-term impact of decisions than on results which might be evident within the period in office. A change in mindset towards the long term may be a challenge for some; not least, it challenges the orthodoxy of the need for leaders to be seen to be doing something. But this approach better reflects the fact that universities do not exist to deliver a quarterly return, or a good year-end result, but need to provide value which outlives any individual. This would also return leadership to a service model, rejecting the heroic leadership approach and prioritising the wellbeing of students, staff, and the institution over the grand gesture or decisive manœuvring.

As well as the executives within universities, governing body members may need to change their approaches. Boards are too often accused of operating with the mindset of a business; this is a useful perspective but may fail to appreciate the need for multi-generational success at the institution. This means assessing performance not just by the size of the surplus or the number of students but with a set of measures on the quality and impact of research, on the outcomes – and not just financial – of the students' education, and on the broader impact on communities. In selecting leaders, boards need to think about how best to achieve a connected set of goals without too much emphasis on one dimension over another. But the reality is that they are not going to find all the qualities they need in one person: if there is one thing above all else that is crucial to success, it is the ability of the vice-chancellor to know when they need advice and support and to ask for it.

Policymakers

Policymakers play a crucial role too. Their decisions, motivated by political, economic, and societal factors, shape the landscape in which universities operate. As we explore the implications of a productised, purpose-driven approach to

HE, we must consider how policymakers can facilitate this transformative shift. One of the most important considerations is value for money. In an era where university education is often perceived as a commodity, ensuring value for money is paramount. However, the evaluation of value must extend beyond merely financial measures. True value in HE encompasses not only the economic returns on investment but also the intellectual, personal, and societal benefits that accrue from a well-rounded education and impactful research. Policymakers must strive to recognise and foster this holistic perspective of value.

There is an undeniable tension between policymakers and universities. Generalised dissatisfaction, fuelled by perceived imbalances in power, often results in an antagonistic relationship. This discord is further exacerbated by a lack of clear, collective vision for the system. Without a shared understanding of the system's overall mission and objectives, collaboration is challenging. Dissatisfaction is deep-seated, encompassing concerns about the individual and collective costs of HE, the quality of outcomes, and the perceived inefficiencies of the system. These issues have led to a crisis of confidence. Restoring faith in the system requires more than just incremental changes; it calls for a significant transformation in how HE is perceived, delivered, and evaluated.

We can safely assume that politically motivated decisions will continue to shape HE policy. After all, universities operate within the social fabric, and their directions are inevitably linked to wider societal aspirations and challenges. Yet, the wish is for a policy environment that seeks value everywhere, not just in the most prestigious institutions or those with the most robust lobbying efforts. Universities of all types and sizes contribute to the richness of the educational ecosystem. Their unique strengths and contributions should be recognised and fostered.

The concept of value should also be expanded to include all forms of education – undergraduate, postgraduate, and lifelong learning – and all facets of a university's mission, including research and enterprise. Policymakers should aim for long-term evaluations which consider the full breadth of a university's impact. While the pressure of short-term political cycles can lead to a focus on immediate outcomes, a longer horizon will allow for a more nuanced and comprehensive assessment of a university's value.

To facilitate a positive transformation, policymakers need to consider several critical factors. First, they should establish a clear vision for the HE system, one which acknowledges its multifaceted purpose and values all contributions. Second, they need to foster a culture of collaboration, encouraging dialogue between stakeholders and seeking to align policies with the realities and aspirations of universities. Third, they must strive for transparency in their decisions and provide robust evidence to support their policy choices. The realisation of the future university depends significantly on the actions of policymakers. By adopting a broad, inclusive, and long-term view of value, fostering collaboration, and championing transparency, policymakers can help facilitate the transition to this new model, ensuring that universities continue to deliver significant benefits for individuals and society.

***

The future university will be populated by people organised in their communities as they are today. There can remain the sense of public purpose within the propositions offered here, even those which push universities to think in a more focussed way about the business model. Not everyone likes the marketised system (in fact, few people would say that it works well), but the primary task is to work within its constraints – typically, what the institution's founding document mandates – rather than fight the system. With a more positive footing, universities can also shape the system, the better to meet their ends. Rather than expending undue effort fighting the system, universities can focus on delivering what is really important, creating value for students and communities.

Postscript | The future university needs imagination

The act of exploring the state, and possible futures, for the HE sector can result in ideas which err on the gloomy side. For those of us immersed in it, day to day, and particularly if we're following the political and media commentary about the sector, it can be a grim place indeed.

If you are inclined to the pessimistic, but have managed to get this far, you might be asking whether any of the proposed reform could ever possibly be achieved. At the heart of the university is a paradox, as Clark Kerr put it in *The Uses of the University*: "Few institutions are so conservative as the universities about their own affairs, while the members are so liberal about the affairs of others; and sometimes the most liberal faculty member in one context is the most conservative in another." With such a weigh of institutional inertia, change is hard.

In recognising that change is hard, but also that it is essential, we need to see the imperative for action at multiple levels. Politicians and policymakers will need to create conditions and incentives for change, including backing institutions seeking to reshape academic careers. University governing bodies will need to review what it means to be successful and ask different questions about how value is created by the institution beyond financial measures. Vice-chancellors and their executives will need to be bold and business-like, focussed on great outcomes across the triple helix of the mission, while ensuring that the university is a place where people are nurtured and supported to achieve their best. This is a subtle balance of head and heart. We should not expect every leader to know this intuitively and therefore we need to support leaders to be their best.

These changes may be hardest in older institutions, typically the more research-intensive. A new settlement on governance may be required which recognises the essential importance of academic voice and leadership but which concedes to the reality that the university needs to be well run for the greater good. Kerr's paradox is real but we need not accept that it prevents us from imagining something better.

***

I hope that in *Higher Imagination* you have found some optimism, some positivity about the value to be found in HE, and how that can be extended and improved. It may be self-evident that HE, just like every other sector, needs to change. While universities exist in part because of the irrational esteem associated with their longevity and social standing, they cannot simply rest on past (or imagined) glories. I, like many others, am confident that HE provides enormous value for its multiple purposes of education, research, and social impact. While there is such opportunity in the value of the sector, it is necessary to adapt to changing conditions, and while it is incumbent on those within and beyond the sector to shape those conditions for the better, the primary task is to work within the constraints provided by the quasi-marketised and highly regulated conditions.

To help prepare the sector for this change, we require imagination. That means to think of ways in which the status quo might be disrupted and to explore potential consequences. This book is an attempt at an imaginative response to the conditions facing the HE sectors in some parts of the world, drawing in particular on direct experiences in the UK and Australian systems. Imagination as thought experiment is one thing, and there are plenty of alternative views on where HE might, or should, go in the future. My approach attempts to bridge those futures to something more here and now; the aspiration is to take imagination and translate it into action.

In the spirit of a dialogic engagement, the invitation is not to adopt that which I have proposed wholesale, but to pick and choose to suit local circumstances. The diversity of institutions and approaches should be a strength for the sector and the source of the experimental approaches from which a lot can be learned.

Dialogue and imagination are necessary, but not sufficient

This book is monologic, and only has meaning when interpreted in the reader's context. It is in that spirit that I have attempted to provide some inspiration, some imagination, as stimulus for the decision making that happens in and around universities. In support of that purpose, I offer some questions to consider:

- What would it mean for your university to place social impact meaningfully alongside education and research within the mission?

- How would you know when the education which your university provides really meets the needs of students?

- How would you ensure that every student can succeed, as well as meeting aggregate success measures?

- What would it take to move to a future where education is seen as a corporate activity for your university?

- How would you support a researcher to articulate the value of their work or area to make the case for investment in them?

- How would you make certain that research investments are equitable across your university, for example across disciplines, and ensure no undue bias?

- How would you know if a university governing body were truly maximising the potential of the institution to deliver on its distinctive mission?

- How would you design your self-optimising university to avoid creating an unwieldy or tyrannical decisions-by-data approach?

- What would it take for your university to be a place in which any and all colleagues can find joy in their work?

The leadership and management of universities is a hard problem, one which thousands of people are pursuing in good faith, trying to do the best they can with limited information about what works best. Norms and conventions are important, and conservatism in decision making is one reason why universities have been so resilient as organisations. The question is when to step back and reimagine the core incentives and structures for how the university is run to see if there is more value to unlock. I think there is.

This book provides a manifesto for change in the sector which pushes some trends to more extreme positions, as in the case of productising education, and introduces balancing concepts, like the promotion of joy, to propose a future university which delivers on its public-purpose mission while achieving good for staff, students, and communities. As a thought experiment, it exists in isolation. When seen as a provocation for dialogue, there is potential for a manifesto to provide tangible value in the work of the HE sector's leaders. I invite you to explore this book, to adopt or reject its concepts, to imagine possible futures and consequences, and to find joy on the journey.

***

www.ingramcontent.com/pod-product-compliance
Lightning Source LLC
Chambersburg PA
CBHW040243010526
44107CB00065B/2852